How To Start Your Own Language Translation & Interpreter Business

The Complete "How-To" Guide for Language Interpreters, Translators and Professionals Starting their own Language Translation Business

Salvador Soto

authorHOUSE®

AuthorHouse™
1663 Liberty Drive
Bloomington, IN 47403
www.authorhouse.com
Phone: 1-800-839-8640

Editorial Director:	*Salvador Soto*
Managing Editor:	*Elizabeth A. Barajas*
Assistant Editor:	*Nichole Rodriguez*
Cover Design:	*Santiago Torres*
Researcher:	*Marlin Garcia*
Research Assistant:	*Don Banowetz*
Research Assistant:	*Jessica Soto*
Production:	*Author House Publications & DeSoto Press*

First published by AuthorHouse 1/20/2010

ISBN: 978-1-4490-5154-9 (sc)

Printed in the United States of America
Bloomington, Indiana

This book is printed on acid-free paper.

Library of Congress Control Number: 2009913717

Available Spring 2010:

The Complete Handbook for the Emerging Business, Political & Community Leader:
The Secrets of Success for Leaders on the Rise

Visit
www.DESOTOTRANSLATIONS.com

ABOUT THE AUTHOR

Salvador "Sal" Soto - *Entrepreneur, Motivational Speaker, Veteran, Consultant, Leader and Author* of *The Handbook for the Emerging Hispanic Leader & How to Start Your Own Translation and Interpreting Business.* Sal started DeSoto Translations (formerly DeSoto Translation & Marketing) in 1999 at the age of 23. Since opening DeSoto Translations Sal has gone on to start several businesses and lead numerous innovative projects.

Sal is the son of Mexican migrant workers. Sal's family traveled throughout the United States, settling in Fort Wayne, Indiana. Growing up poor and Hispanic in the Midwest had several challenges. *"We didn't speak English well and the locals didn't speak Spanish at all- so communicating for our family was a huge struggle."*

Sal dropped out of school twice but somehow managed to graduate with his H.S. diploma. Sal went on to college but he wasn't sure what he wanted to do with his life and money was tight. *"I enlisted in the Navy to get my life in perspective. From the first day of boot camp I realized that what I really wanted was to be back at school."* Sal was stationed in Texas, California & the Middle East before being discharged. After leaving the Navy Sal hit the books hard, working during the day and attending college at night and weekends. Sal received his college degree from the University of Saint Francis with concentrations in business and social work and plans to get his MBA.

At the age of 23 Sal had a prominent job (Director of Diversity Initiatives at the United Way), but it just wasn't enough. There had to be something more out there that was a better fit. That something more ended up being the birth of his company-DeSoto Translations. *"With $500 and a dream I launched my company and never looked back."*

In 2007 DeSoto Translations received several awards and accolades and Sal was individually recognized by Hispanic Business Magazine as one of the *Entrepreneurs of the Year (EOY) in the "Rising Star" Category.* Sal was the runner-up but was humbled by the experience. *"It was nice to be recognized by such a prestigious group and to be recognized by my peers."* Sal said of his award nomination.

Notable Awards & Recognitions

2008 Indiana Companies to Watch

2007 Hispanic Business Magazine (EOY) Entrepreneur of the Year "Rising Star" Runner-Up

2006 & 2007 United States Junior Chamber Semi-finalist Ten Outstanding Young Americans Award

2007 FW Business Weekly Innovation Award Winner

2007 Innovator of the Year Award- FW Business Weekly- Finalist

2005 Future 40 Leaders under 40- FW Business Journal

2004 Chamber of Commerce (Indiana) "Diversity Business of the Year"

2004 Indiana Governors Award for Tomorrow's Leaders

1999 Dr. Juan Andrade Scholarship for Hispanic Leaders

Sal has found a new calling providing start-up and trademark licensing assistance to DeSoto Translation representatives and licensees. In 2009, Sal started a new company, DeSoto Holdings, LLC., as the umbrella company for his businesses and initiatives. Additionally, Sal is providing motivational/keynote speaking and consultation services - speaking across the country on such topics as Entrepreneurship, Emerging Leadership, The Growing Latino Community, Starting Your Own Language Business and Building Creative Communities. Visit Sal on the web at **www.SALSOTO.com** for more information and speaking requests.

DEDICATION

This book is dedicated to my family, friends, staff, clients and mentors for all your support, motivation and inspiration.

AUTHORS ACKNOWLEDGMENTS

This book would not be possible without the help and support of some key people who have been in my life over the years. Although everyone that comes in my life has helped me in some way shape or form (even if they didn't know it) I am especially thankful to my parents for doing the best they could with the little they had and for teaching me the importance of respect and hard work.

Dr. Juan Andrade, President of the United States Hispanic Leadership Institute (USHLI) for believing in me before I believed in myself. Alfredo Perez and Carlos Ramos, my first official mentors for their encouragement, friendship and inspiration. My sincerest appreciation to Steve Corona, John Dortch and Larry Rowland- my unofficial Advisory Board and Consigliore's for their advice, guidance and friendship.

Ben Campbell, Don Schenkel, Jesus Chavarria, Jorge Ferraez, Henry Cisneros, John Hanna, Tony Lopez, Jerry Peterson, Dr. David Abalos, Sen. David Long, Sen. Tom Wyss, Bill Brown, Matt Faley, Frank Byrne, Michelle Gladieux, Mark Outlaw, Kim Waldschmidt, Luther Whitfield, Al Stoller, Matt Schomburg, Marc Levy, Bob Anderson and Willie Jordan for their help and support over the years. Lyman Lewis from the IPFW School of Business & IPFW MBA students Blaine Hershberger, Bridget Matthes, Lauren Wilson and Brad Hittle for their hard work and research on this project. And everyone else that has helped me along the way....I wish all of you the best in your future endeavors.

To all those that I have had the pleasure to work with over the years especially Monica Klug, Emily Schwartz-Keirns, Elizabeth A. Barajas, Alejo & Santiago Torres, Jeremy Mangin, Angie Soto-Phillips, Don Banowetz, Jose Cruz, Emily, Rico & Aaron Guerrero, Marlin & Edna Garcia, Nichole Rodriguez, Hector Mercedes, Chad Pollitt, Paul Rodriguez ... I'm Sorry if I drove you crazy.

I want to thank my 5 brothers and sisters, my extended family and my close friends. Last, but not least, my wife, Jessica and my daughters Isabellla, Olivia and Ava for making me laugh when I need one, keeping me grounded when my head is in the clouds and for keeping me sane when things are going crazy. Words cannot express how much you all mean to me. Thank you!

Contents

FOREWORD

The Story of Me & My Four Bosses

If you are reading this book you are probably where I was back in the fall of 1999. The economy was on a downward spiral eventually ending in a recession in part because of the crash of the Dot-Com market and the tragic events in New York on 9/11 sealed the deal. I was in a job that paid well, but for some reason I was not happy. I did what most of us do, I stopped complaining and started accepting that this was how things were in the "real world" and if I didn't have a better way to pay my car loan than I had better deal with it.

As I began to look at the job market I found that there wasn't much out there in my field, at least nothing nearby that paid as well as the job I had. I began an intensive job hunt. Just a short time into my search I decided that I just couldn't do it anymore- I had to quit my job. Besides making me unhappy I think that it was making me physically sick. Did I mention that I had four bosses at my current job? Two who were driving me crazy and the other two spent much of their time apologizing for the others.

It was a rainy day in September when I sat in front of my computer and typed the most important letter of my life: *"Dear Bosses, Effective (some date in the near future) I will no longer be an employee of this company. Thank you for the opportunity."* I placed one letter on my direct supervisor's desk and sent out an e-mail to my entire company so that I couldn't change my mind. As people began to ask me where I was going I had to answer with a shaky yet confident, *"I am not sure, but I am excited at the opportunities ahead of me."*

The opportunities at the time were none. The very next day reality set in, I just quit my job and I didn't have another job lined up, as a matter of fact I hadn't even sent out one resume. I immediately went from excited to terrified, "What have I done?"

Over the following months I went on several interviews that didn't lead to much, but I was staying optimistic since I still had a few more weeks at my current job. There was a "Direct-Marketing" company that I had interviewed with extensively and it was looking very promising. I had my reservations about the company but I put them aside because this was the only company with a pending offer and my current job was about to end.

I was given an offer and asked to come in for one more "live" interview to see the business first hand. I arrived at the company office and instructed to ride with some of the "area managers" for convenience to participate in a live marketing campaign "Kick-Off" for a client. We drove for a while before I realized we were no longer in the city — far from phones and stores which made me a bit nervous, this was before cell phones were affordable to the common man. We pulled up to a neighborhood that was still under construction on the outskirts of a city about 40 miles away from the "corporate office." As soon as we parked our vehicles I got a gut feeling that something was wrong. *"Grab a backpack and make sure that it's got the coupons we are selling today."* the manager yelled out to everyone.

It was at that very moment that I realized that they…we… were door to door salesmen. We were selling coupons for a local pizza parlor they had "partnered" with. *"Oh My God, I can't believe I fell for this."* To make things worse, we were out in the middle of nowhere and I was stuck walking around with these guys for the entire day until they could drive me home. That morning I witnessed some of the tackiest, rudest and borderline illegal sales tactics ever. I called a friend from a gas station while we were on a pit stop and begged him to pick me up before I went crazy or got arrested for being with these people.

A few days after that incident was my last day of work and during a conversation with my soon-to-be ex-boss he asked me if I found another job. I told him that I had not found a new job yet. This is where the conversation got really interesting, my boss said, *"What about the Spanish translation and interpreting projects you've been coordinating for our client's? Is there any money in doing that? At least it will keep you out of trouble while you look for another job."* And the rest as they say is history.

"The No. 1 thing people can do to increase their wealth is start a part-time business"

—**Robert Kiyosaki**
Author of *Rich Dad Poor Dad*

COMPANY OVERVIEW
The Restaurant Owner Who Couldn't Cook

I initially shrugged off the idea of starting my own translation and interpreting business since my Spanish wasn't the greatest and I went to college for social work not business or Spanish. However, I thought about this idea very seriously and since I am Hispanic, both my parents are Mexican, it sounded like a good idea. But I was raised in Indiana most of my life and my Spanish was "rusty" to say the very least. Growing up we were encouraged to speak English at home and not allowed to speak Spanish in school. On top of that, I never did well with written Spanish once I enrolled in courses, so how was I going to provide Spanish translation and interpreting services let alone run a full-service language company?

I spent the next several months researching the translation & interpreting industry and even visited several agencies to see first-hand how I could set up a similar company. One of the key things that I realized while researching the industry was that the larger translation companies were headed up by individuals that were either monolingual or barley bilingual but had strong business and problem solving skills allowing them to provided a wide array of languages & services and the smaller businesses ("mom & pop shops") were led by bilingual (usually one language) individuals and had a very small focus of services (ex. Spanish only legal documents) and a very limited client base.

I liked the full-service model, especially since I needed to focus my time and energy developing the company and client base. I would be like a restaurant owner who couldn't cook. My job would be to hire the best chefs and use the highest quality ingredients to ensure satisfaction. Since I couldn't speak or write Spanish well I was going to have to come up with a system or process to ensure accuracy and quality and have a system for checking projects regardless of the language. I went to work on developing this new process, researching various industries for models that could be copied and adapted to my needs. It was actually in my old job as a proofreader for Columbia House Records (The cd's for a penny people) and researching deaf and sign language interpreters that I found a model that would become the basis of our system for delivery, accuracy and quality.

After about a year of development I had fine-tuned the process I'd been searching for and began using it on a small scale for Spanish interpreting and translation projects. My first clients for large scale interpreting and translation services were intense and in retrospect very challenging. One of my first clients was a health system that approached me and asked if we could provide on-site language interpreting services 24-hrs a day to all of their facilities (9 in four different cities) in multiple languages year-round? Another client was a major automotive company that needed their quality assurance manual (600 page technical manual) translated from English to Portuguese. Finally, there was a court system that needed court interpreters that spoke Russian, Bosnian, Japanese, Burmese, French, Spanish and German that could be available at various locations on an "emergency basis." Emergency notice was equivalent to 15-30 minutes.

To meet these demands we would go through practice drills of calling interpreters to evaluate their response times and which routes were the fastest to get to our destination. We had heated debates over the usage and correct translation of certain words and phrases. There were even conversations and arguments with clients over the translation projects we provided to them because someone at their company was "bilingual" and thought our translation was not translated correctly. Almost every company had someone that was the unofficial "bilingual" person that would give the final review and approval on the translation projects we were submitting. After discussing the project with these "bilingual" individuals over and over about the same thing we created a few rules to provide both parties with an outline of what to expect from us and what we would need from them for the project to be a success.

Translation Project- Reciprocal Rules and Responsibilities

- Personal preference does not mean it is incorrect, everything can be said differently.

- When it comes to writing; Not all correct writing is good...

- And not all good writing is correct!

- Whoever knows the rule wins (grammar and language rules)

- Unless the client has asked us to localize the translation for a certain country/ region it is our job to make recommendations and the client's job to pick colloquial terms, words, phrases, & preferences for words that do not exist in certain languages and/or industries, etc.

- We do not "dumb down" projects. To assume the education or reading level of the entire target audience is low could be considered an insult.

- The client is ultimately right, even if that means the translation will be incorrect. (I would ask that your company not be associated with the project if this is the case).

- Put your team and/or process against claims (mistakes, errors, etc.) that you are incorrect or that the project is not translated accurately at all times. (Keep in mind, we are human and mistakes happen, so review the project before arguing this point. Only after you have investigated the issue would I ask for a meeting to clarify your findings.)

Remember this is business and it is in your best interests to approach these types of meetings and conversations with courtesy and respect. If the "bilingual" individuals were fluent enough to proofread or translate the project, then why was the project outsourced? There will be occasions where you will need to meet with the supervisor or executive overseeing the project to explain your translation process and the specifics of the translation if the "bilingual" person or project team you are meeting with is not willing to accept your translation. Some people, for whatever reason (pride, ego, etc.), do not want to admit when they have made a mistake or when they are wrong. However, you are ultimately responsible for the accuracy and overall quality of the project. Protect your reputation at all times.

Since its inception, my company has provided Globalization, Internationalization, Localization and Translation (GILT) services as well as language interpreters 24 hours a day for a countless number of murder trials, custody battles, surgeries, cancer treatments, FBI investigations, federal court drug cases and more. Our clients include Fortune 100 & 500 companies planning to go international or with an established international market and business. What started as a company to "keep me busy and out of trouble" has flourished into a successful international business.

The Future for DeSoto Translations

I have always had an eye for identifying and capitalizing on opportunities. With that in mind, my company is now focused on providing language translation franchising and trademark license services to help interpreters, foreign language professionals and entrepreneurs start their own language translation businesses. We have also opened a consultation division to assist our representatives and language translation companies develop their own internal language translation & interpreter networks. Visit us on the web to learn more at: www.desototranslations.com or www.salsoto.com.

"Efforts and courage are not enough without purpose and direction."

— **John F. Kennedy**
U.S. President & Leader

PURPOSE OF THIS BOOK

What Drives You?

What we set out to do with this book was to create a "how-to" resource for language business owners and entrepreneurs that needed assistance and guidance in doing what we did back in 1999, start and manage their own language translation and interpreting business. However, we want people to start where we have left off, not where we started 10 years ago. There is no need to re-create the wheel or to make the same mistakes we made when starting out in the industry.

This book will help you focus and understand the "business" side of the language industry. We have provided the reader with tools, resources and set the reader in the right direction to start the business they have always dreamed of successfully. Whether you are a for-profit company looking to expand, a one-person "freelancer" looking for an edge in the industry or a not for profit organization interested in creating a language translation & interpreting network, this book has been developed to assist you in navigating the "ins & outs" of the linguistics industry from a business perspective.

Working with veterans and recently developed language translation businesses we have created the first and only resource in the marketplace today that will assist you as you create your language translation & interpreting business using real examples, processes, fee structures and tips that have proven to work successfully in "The Real World." The language industry is here, growing just as the global market continues to grow by leaps and bounds. When starting my company I didn't always hit homeruns and I wish I had learned my mistakes with someone else's money.

As a successful mentor and businessman once told me, *"You have to pay to get your education."* You can take what we learned and apply it to your business so you don't repeat our mistakes.

There's one final thought I'd like to leave you with, remember this is a business that you will need to invest not just time and money, but your patience, understanding and love. Yes, love.

"If you work doing something you love,
you will never work a day in your life."
- Unknown

To ensure this book was up-to-date we gave several copies away for review, consulted with those who had read the book and met with companies using actual methods and processes from the book. We have worked out the bugs by taking this book around the country to try out with actual companies, language program coordinators and language translation businesses to ensure that the concepts in this book would work across the country.

We have also created a website for support and questions as well as forms, agreements, Ready-To-Use Rate Sheets and much more. Feel free to leave us your comments and ideas on what you like to see in future editions and publications.

Visit us at www.desototranslations.com for more resources.

DeSoto Translations has provided translation services and language interpreters in over 50 languages over the years in some of the most unfortunate of circumstances. Since there were no protocols or rules to follow we had to create them as we went along. I will admit that starting a business is a bit intimidating and somewhat overwhelming. But as with anything time and practice will help you past these fears and anxieties. Look at it this way; at least you are starting with over 15 years+ of award-winning expertise, knowledge, and resources, which is a lot more than most of us in the industry started with.

After ten years in business, several awards and over a million dollars later I felt it was the right time to share the concepts, strategies and practical business ideas that have made my company and myself a success.

I sincerely wish you the best in reaching your dreams and aspirations.

"If You Are Going to Dream, Dream Big"
- Salvador "Sal" Soto

"Excellence can be obtained if you:
Care more than others think is wise;
Risk more than others think is safe;
Dream more than others think is practical
Expect more than others think is possible."

— *Unknown*

WHAT THIS BOOK IS NOT

Does it Work Underwater?

I wanted to make sure that readers understand what the purpose of this book is as well as what it is not. This book is intended to assist the reader in creating a language translation & interpreting BUSINESS. There are several books, resources, schools, trainings and programs that focus on becoming a better interpreter and/or translator. We have listed several resources (dictionaries, etiquette guides and medical & legal terminology books) as well as websites in the back of this book that you can visit to help you become a better language interpreter and/or translator.

If you would like to become a certified language interpreter/translator (state, federal or private) in a specific language or industry (medical, court, technical) check out the list of resources in the back of the book or visit our website for the most up-to-date list of resources, testing locations and registration fees.

Website address: www.desototranslations.com

There are several methods, processes and models you can use to achieve similar results in creating your language interpreting & translation business. We encourage you to use what you know and what works for you. As a friend use to always say to me, "There's more than one way to skin a cat."

Additionally, you will meet people along the way that will argue that you have to be from the country you are providing services (Chinese Translation company must have a Chinese CEO) or that you have to have this certification or that degree or be affiliated with certain associations to be credible or successful.

Pay these people no mind. These are usually the ramblings of your competitors trying to scare you off or scare potential clients from using your company because of some subjective irrelevant reason (which is very unprofessional). Instead of joining in or defending yourself, offer your services for free on occasion to get yourself out there, mention some recent achievements as a measure of your credibility (awards for service/quality) when meeting with clients or news reporters or simply take the high road and not respond to your critics or competitors.

Focus on getting clients that your competitor doesn't want or that are not in their area of expertise (ex. hospitals in the middle of nowhere in need of Spanish translation services) to avoid directly competing for clients with a more established competitor at the initial start-up of your business. I have always believed that actions speak louder than words. As your client base grows, so will your credibility, expertise and business skills. If you have no competition I am happy for you…however, just as you realized the language industry is a growing market with endless opportunities, it will not take long for others to follow suit and try to ride your coat-tails using the hard work and foundation you have laid down to their advantage.

There are three things I have learned in business:

1. Business is like a game.
2. Protect yourself at all times.
3. Some people don't play fair.

I recommend taking on-going classes, workshops and trainings whenever possible on small business and small business management. The rule of thumb that I have learned is that once I have learned to do something (accounting, sales, marketing, website design, etc.) there is a faster, cheaper and more efficient way of doing things that I will have to get more information or training on to figure out how it all works together.

Whenever possible use agreements and contracts to protect not only your assets, business, property and interests but that of the other party. I'm not saying to give the other party the upper hand in a deal but I am saying it is never a good thing to only look out for one's own interests or to exploit the weaknesses of the other party. Be ethical, fair and reasonable in business and expect the same in return.

However, there will be those out there that are not playing by the same rules and will do whatever they can and want as long as it is in their best interests. None of us likes to think that our new employee or client will steal from us or that a good friend or family member would ever take advantage of you. I wish I could say that it didn't happen to me or that I was smart enough to not get taken by someone's lies, but I too have made these mistakes and that is partly why I am writing this book. (Read more in Ch. 22- Protecting Your ASSet's)

> *"Beware a wolf in sheep's clothing!"*
> *- Aesop's Fables*

"By working faithfully eight hours a day you may eventually get to be the boss and work twelve hours a day."

— Robert Frost
Poet

IS THIS BUSINESS FOR ME?

What is your Mission & What makes you Unique

When I first got into the translation & interpreting business I had no clue all the facets and levels involved in the process, all I knew was that I was just one part of the communication chain. Once I realized this I started looking within my company to see where we could provide additional services and support. As you look within yourself and begin to asses your skills and resources keep in mind that one of the best things about being a small business is that you can be flexible and change direction and focus as needed. If something doesn't work you can scrap it and if an opportunity presents itself you can grab it.

As the owner and president of the company I spend most of my time creating processes, policies and procedures for the way things should be done for my company and clients. I spend even more time making sure that the things I created work and fine tuning the areas that could work better. If you do not like problem solving, foreign languages and working with people then I would seriously reconsider entering the linguistics industry.

The successful language industry business owner likes the constant challenges, opportunities, and flexibility to create solutions as well as the similarities & diversity of cultures. There are several ways that certain phrases and words can be translated and still be correct. Working with your clients you will be making recommendations along with the proofreader and/or translator and explaining the reasoning behind these recommendations to your client.

If you do not speak the language at all (ex. full-service language company CEO's) you will be the customer service representative that will work with your clients to choose from the recommendations provided and spend a lot of time identifying and selling your services to clients and companies in need of your services.

A common mistake that a lot of small business owners, entrepreneurs and "freelancers" make when taking the company to the next level is that they believe that they need to go big (big office, big clients, big staff, etc.) or that the new company structure needs to be this complex and elaborate thing. My advice is to take it slow and let nature take its course. Going big for the sake of going big doesn't help anyone in the long run and in a slow economy could be a waste of capital needed for sustainability until the market picks up. Grow as needed when needed.

Another mistake that business owners make is thinking that they cannot be successful unless the business looks and works exactly like they envisioned it. An "All or Nothing" concept should be debunked at the beginning of your business or you will be fighting with yourself the entire time you are in business… a businesses that may never meet your expectations.

Appreciate and enjoy the start-up phase. This is where you will fine-tune your price, product and the delivery of your services. You will also learn how to do things you are not good at so that when the time arises you will be able to perform the tasks needed or know where to find the answers in a crunch. You will have established great staff members, dependable vendors and appreciative clients that you can trust which is an accomplishment you would never have achieved if you tried to "Run before you could walk."

Most successful businesses didn't start out doing what they do now, most busineses go through several stages and set-backs to get where they are today. Here are some common excuses I've heard as to why the business person has not started their business: *"I can't do what I wanted because I didn't get the client I wanted."* I'm sure you've heard this one…*"If I only had 1 million dollars in start-up money I know we could make this project work." "If I could just get Wal-mart as a client I will be set."*

I'm sure that with 1 million dollars or Wal-mart as a client most projects would be a success. The reality is you don't have a million dollars (yet) and Wal-mart is not a client (yet) so you will need to figure out how to make this work where you are at so that when you do get the call from the Wal-mart or an investor you can show them how you were able to turn obstacles and challenges into successes and profits. The last thing anyone wants to hear is excuses, so don't make any.

"To be prepared is half the victory"
Miguel De Cervantes

There are several business structures and business structure combinations that you could use as your business model. Here are some common business structures you will see in the Language Industry

Language Industry Business Models

- One person "freelancer"
- Not-for-profit program
- Volunteer Interpreter Network
- Full-service Translation Company
- Interpreting only
- Translation only
- Home-based
- Major corporation clients
- 24-hour Services
- On-site Only
- Phone Only
- Emergency Appointments
- Scheduled Appointments
- General Translations
- Walk-ins
- Business to Business
- Court Interpreting Only
- …..and this goes on.

It is up to you as to when, where, why, how your company provides services and at what rate or fee you will charge. I advise you to think very carefully about all your costs before you put out your rates or just start charging a little less than what your competitors are charging. You may have more overhead, start-up costs and staff than they do and if you do not take these things into account when you calculate (or adopt the rates suggested in this book) your rates you could put yourself out of business.

Mission Statement & Unique Value Proposition Statement

To focus on what your new or current company mission is (and is not) you will want to create a brief mission statement. In this statement you will outline in a very succinct sentence or paragraph why you started your business and what it will accomplish. In this day and age many people feel that mission statements have become irrelevant. With the speed of decisions and change that occurs so quickly, many executives say that mission statements are too confining, they lack the fluidity that is necessary to compete in a fast paced world and are window dressing that have no value. To those people, I simply ask them to "think again." Mission Statements, if crafted correctly, are the cornerstone to an effective strategy. Mission Statements that are short, memorable and uniting can help all team members within an organization stay true to why that business exists.

Here are some of the qualities that I have found in Great Mission's

The statement is short. Less than 10 words and easy to remember.

The statement answers the question, "Why does our company exist?"

It is used to make big decisions. So when someone in a meeting says, "Hold on, we are too in weeds, let's step back and look at the big picture." The mission statement can be referenced to provide clarity of direction and decision making.

The mission statement is genuine and "lived." Meaning that the culture of the company is in-line with its "essence." So when a Googler thinks about a new product or service - they can test it against - "Does this, Do No Evil?" And if it does no evil then it is in alignment.

The company should be on a mission not just have a well written, verbose mission statement. So when Merck sets out to preserve and improve human life - that is a mission that people can support.

It should be communicated often and should be easy to find within any office of the company.

It should appear in all annual reports and strategic communications.

It should be used in the hiring process to help identify candidates that can aid in its accomplishment.

It should stand the test of time (20 years is a good length). If you can look at your mission statement and say 20 years from today we will still be focused on that "end" - then you have a solid foundation.

It should be a worthwhile aim. Mission statements that lack passion, importance and relevance to employees, clients and shareholders aren't worth the effort it takes to create and communicate them.

With these qualities stated, here are some tips to create a great Mission:

Ask your team (or yourself if it is just you) this question – "Why do we exist?" Challenge them to think about this from an employee, client, shareholder and the general public at large standpoint.

Capture consistent themes that convey passion. For example, "To save lives;" "To share knowledge;" "To educate;" "To enhance;" "To simplify;" "To enrich." These are all very brief ideas that convey a worthy effort.

Have your team (or advisors) rank the top 3 themes and find the one that stands above all else.

Challenge them to consider if this ideal will be relevant 20 years from now.

Once you have narrowed it down - have someone document it in 10 words or less. Take some time to let it marinate and come back to it to see if it is correct.

Once you are committed to it - then share it with the entire organization. Put it on your web site, your office walls, letterhead, etc. I know a few companies that start meetings with a reading of their mission statement.

Use it to make decisions.

Annually challenge your team to question where they are falling short of achievement toward its end.

Live it

Here are some examples of great Mission Statement

- Disney - To make people happy

- Google - To do no evil

- Merck - To preserve and improve human life

- Mary Kay - To give unlimited opportunity to women

Note: Parts of the above lists were adapted from a report by CeoWise, "Strategic Planning-Mission Statements" 2007

"*Observe all men; thy self most.*"

— **Benjamin Franklin**
Scientist, Writer & Politician

ENTREPRENEURIAL QUIZ

I Can Do My Own Taxes, but I'd Rather Pay H&R Block

It is important to know your strengths and weaknesses so that you can work on areas of weakness and take full advantage of your strengths. I encourage you to take this simple Entrepreneur Quiz to assess your likes and dislikes related to areas you will be expected to address as an entrepreneur and/or business owner. What you will find is that there will be some things you will need to compensate for if they are things you do not like to do or do not do well (ex. making sales calls, doing paperwork, balancing the finances or meeting with new clients). You will also identify your strengths which you can focus your energy in maximizing and outsource or delegate those things you'd prefer not to do. Due to limited funds at the onset of your business you may have no choice but to do everything on your own. However, as the business grows you can set aside money to pay for the services you would like to outsource.

		Yes	No	Sometimes
1.	I am a self-starter. Nobody has to tell me how to get going	_____	_____	_____
2.	I am capable of getting along with just about everybody.	_____	_____	_____
3.	I have no trouble getting people to follow my lead.	_____	_____	_____
4.	I like to be in charge of things and see them through.	_____	_____	_____
5.	I always plan ahead before beginning a project. I am usually the one who gets everyone organized	_____	_____	_____
6.	I have a lot of stamina. I can keep going as long as necessary.	_____	_____	_____
7.	I have no trouble making decisions and can make up my mind in a hurry	_____	_____	_____
8.	I say exactly what I mean. People can trust me.	_____	_____	_____

9. Once I make my mind up to do something, nothing can stop me.

_____   _____   _____

10. I am in excellent health and have a lot of energy.

_____   _____   _____

11. I have experience or Technical knowledge in the business I intend to start.

_____   _____   _____

12. I feel comfortable taking risks if it is something I really believe in

_____   _____   _____

13. I have good communication skills

_____   _____   _____

14. I am flexible in my dealings with people and situations

_____   _____   _____

15. I consider myself creative and resourceful.

_____   _____   _____

16. I can analyze a situation and take steps to correct problems.

_____   _____   _____

17. I think I am capable of maintaining a good working relationship with employees.

_____   _____   _____

18. I am not a dictator. I am willing to listen to employees, customers and suppliers

_____   _____   _____

19. I'm not rigid in my policies. I'm willing to adjust to meet the needs of employees, customers.

_____   _____   _____

20. More than anything else, I want to run my own business.

_____   _____   _____

Totals   _____   _____   _____

If the total of Column #1 is the highest, then you will probably be very successful in running your own business.

If the total of column #2 is the highest, you may find that running a business is more than you can handle.

If the total of Column #3 is the highest, you should consider taking on a partner who is strong in your weak areas.

NOTE: This quiz was adapted from the Small Business Administration publication checklist for "Going into Business."

"If language is not correct, then what is said is not what is meant; if what is said is not what is meant, then what must be done remains undone; if this remains undone, morals and art will deteriorate; if justice goes astray, the people will stand about in helpless confusion. Hence there must be no arbitrariness in what is said. This matters above everything."

-Confucius

Chapter 1
HOW MANY LANGUAGES ARE THERE?

It's All Greek to Me

Translators and interpreters represent two key segments of the "linguistics" industry. They facilitate the cross-cultural communication necessary in today's global society. Being effective at the task requires more than converting one language to another- translators and interpreters must also grasp and relay the social concepts behind the text or spoken words. They need to thoroughly comprehend the topics upon which their work focuses, so they can accurately convey information and ideas from one language (known in the industry as the "source language") to another (the "target language").

Translation is a written process. Services include translation of legal, medical and business documents from one language to another. Translation of Internet websites and documentation of hardware and software are growing niches as well. Interpretation is a spoken process. Interpreters provide the necessary communication between people who speak different languages, or between hearing impaired (sign language). Interpreters work in one-on-one settings as well as in situations requiring simultaneous interpretations (for example, large gatherings like the United Nations, and presentations to audiences that speak many different languages). In recent years the translation & interpreting industry has been described using the following terms: Globalization, Internationalization, Localization and Translation. This has led to the usage of the acronym (GILT) when describing any or all of the above services.

Translations & Interpreters in History

The early history of language interpreting and translation can be traced back to religion. One of the first important translations was of the Old Testament from Hebrew to Greek. A historical group of translations referred to as *Septuagint* (sĕp'tōō-ā-jĭnt') from seventy or "The Seventy" (70) in Latin, was given to this text translation to acknowledge the seventy or so Jewish scholars that completed the translation in seventy-two days in Alexandria sometime in the 3rd century B.C.. The scholars completed the translation so the dispersed Jews who had forgotten their ancestral language would have a translation of their scriptures.

Along with religion, translations in the areas of literature and poetry were being translated into English from Italian and Latin during the same period. However, translations and the interpretations of religious texts were extremely complex but also very important in history. Controversy over certain words brought divides between religions and hatred towards some. One of the most famous stories in the history of religion and language is the story of The Tower of Babel.

The Tower of Babel

The Tower of Babel is a story from Genesis in the bible that centers on an enormous tower in the city of Babel (now thought to be Babylon). According to the story, the people of Babel became skilled in construction and decided to build a city with a tower that would reach to the heavens. By building the tower they wanted to make a name for themselves and come together so they would not be scattered throughout the world. God came to see their city and the tower they were building. He perceived their intentions as selfish ambition, not for the worshiping of God, and in His infinite wisdom, He felt this "stairway to heaven" would only lead the people away from God.

As a result, God confused their language, causing them to speak different languages so they would not understand each other. By doing this, God thwarted their plans to finish their tower. He also scattered the people of Babel all over the face of the earth. It is believed that this is where the phrase "You're babbling" was derived.

Language Translation & History

Throughout history translations of documents and books from one language to another have been completed. According to United Bible Societies, as of December 31, 2007, the entire Bible had been translated into at least 438 languages, and at least some portion of the Bible had been translated into at least 2,454 languages.

Another document and publisher that has been translated extensively is software giant Microsoft. Microsoft with their software and Help files, beats out many of its rivals as having the most translated documents. With all of the operating systems and Microsoft software programs that have been written and localized and/or translated over the past 20 years, and the translated Help files going out in the majority of computers sold daily.....it will be a long time until another company can compete with this accomplishment. However, Shakespeare, Agatha Christie, Stephen King, Mark Twain, Alexandre Dumas, Hermann Hess, and the Greek Philosopher Plato can all say that they have been translated in just as many languages if not more than Microsoft.

Language Interpreters & History

The Story of Sacajawea

In May of 1804, Meriwether Lewis and William Clark set out to explore and map the American West. President of the United States, Thomas Jefferson commissioned Lewis to head an expedition to explore the newly bought Louisiana Territory with the purpose for furthering trade. Lewis chose his childhood friend Clark as the co-captain of the expedition. Lewis and Clark were accompanied by a crew of men, and later, a Shoshone Indian guide and interpreter Sacajawea (also spelled Sacagawea) as well as her husband and their infant son.

Sacajawea and her husband were hired for the expedition as interpreters to ensure that that the group could communicate with the Indian tribes they would encounter. Although Sacajawea did not speak English, she spoke Shoshone and Hidatsa while her husband spoke Hidatsa and French. According to Clark's documented journals, Sacajawea and her husband became an interpreting team.

In an example of their translating skills, Clark explained that when they met the Shoshones, Sacajawea would talk with them, and then translate to Hidatsa for her husband, who would then translate to French. Francois Labiche, one of the members of the expedition spoke French and English. Labiche would make the final translations so the two English-speaking captains would understand.

Interpreting skills would also make it possible for the group to trade for horses which they needed to cross the mountains. In the summer of 1805, Lewis and Clark's expedition party was spotted heading toward the Continental Divide by a group of Shoshone Indians. The Chief of the tribe turned out to be Sacajawea's brother. Because of Sacajawea's interpreting skills through the chain of captains, the expedition was then able to purchase the horses it needed.

The members of the Lewis and Clark Expedition were the first U.S. citizens to see the Rocky Mountains, cross the continent, and reach the Pacific Ocean. The successful expedition strengthened U.S. claims to the Pacific Northwest, spurred westward expansion, and established good relations with most of the Indian tribes they met. With the assistance of one of the most famous interpreters, the American West was now open to the people of the United States

In Summary

According to a 2007 University of Pennsylvania Department of Linguistics report, there are approximately 6,900 official "living" languages in the world today. The Globalization, Internationalization, Localization and Translation (GILT) Industry that includes language interpretation is an ever-growing industry with infinite opportunity. "Going Global" is no longer a catch-phrase; it is a way of life. Every day we interact and play our part in the global economy, the coffee we drink in the morning is from South America, the car we drive is from Germany, the gas in our car is imported from Saudi Arabia, our laptops are from China with micro-processors from Indonesia and the high-definition flat screen TV's we watch before we go to bed are from Japan.

Within all these importing and exporting transactions are interpreters and translations taking manuals, documents, agreements and conversations from one language to another. If there is a breakdown in the communication chain a communication breakdown will occur and commerce will cease, leading to millions-billions of dollars in losses and lost opportunities. That is why language interpreters and those interested in the GILT industry are in such high demand.

Depending on what language you are translating; the same language may translate very differently between countries. Words and their meanings can change based on the location that they are used. Some of the literal translations are not so nice, mistranslating the word or meaning to become something offensive. Keeping the meaning and message of the original document or source text in the translation process becomes more of an art form than an exact science.

Today, Interpreters and translations are being used in all areas of daily life, from helping enroll a student into a new school to assisting in the heart surgery of a Russian speaking patient to interpreting for a corporate executive that has just purchased a new business in another country. Because language is continually changing it will be years before there is a computer program intelligent enough to translate and comprehend as well as a human. Thus, ensuring job security in the language translation and interpreting industry for years to come.

"Luck is what happens when preparation meets opportunity."

- **Seneca**
Roman Philosopher

Chapter 2
MARKET OVERVIEW
So is There Opportunity Here?

Before going into a business it is important to know how much you can expect to make with the endeavor and how large the industry is or is expected to be. Size estimates of the translation and interpretation industry have only become available within the last decade because governments have only recently begun to collect such information and only recently have some companies grown large enough to divulge such information to the public.

While *Language Line* ® is one of the most familiar names in the industry with offices world-wide and millions in revenue, as well as thousands of employees and linguists internationally, there are thousands of small to mid-size translation and interpreters employed in-house by large corporations, but the vast majority freelance through agencies or work independently.

Most freelancers and agencies specialize in either translation or interpretation, but some offer both as well as language consultation services. More recently independent freelancers have turned to creating "Full-Service" agencies, outsourcing and contracting services they themselves cannot do.

The information on the exact revenue the linguistics industry brings in has not been made available simply because most translation and interpretation agencies are privately held and don't want to give up their information. Most translation businesses are small to medium sized businesses that started out as a one man/ or woman operation. In their defense, if every other translation company knows what one charges or brings in, they will try to beat out each other and the industry will become overly competitive based on rates not on quality, accuracy or other important factors.

The industry's dynamic growth creates some potential problems when finding data not only because it is growing at such a rapid pace, but with little to no barriers to start up your own company, new agencies are popping up all over the place. New technology also makes numbers skewed because — do you count a human assisted by a machine be classified as machine translation or human translation? How is the industry defined? What I can tell you is that however it is defined, it is growing by leaps and bounds.

In the 1980's it was estimated that $10 to $20 million a year was spent on translation and/or interpreting services. With the influx of new arrivals to the U.S. and the advent of the internet and the increase in businesses advertising globally during the 1990's the estimates were realized. The internet boost also brought about many different assumptions as to what the translation industry brings in. Estimations are simply all over the map. Currently we are nationally looking at a $5 billion to $6 billion industry that is expected to rise to $10 billion by 2013.

Market Leaders

Company	Revenue	Offices
Lionbridge Technologies	$400 million	50
L-3	$372 million	n/a*
Transperfect/Translations	$74 million	30
SDI Media Group**	$65 million	23
Merrill Brink International	$24.5 million	4
McNeil Multilingual	$24.3 million	5

Projected U.S. Language Services Revenue
(By Year, in Billions of Dollars)

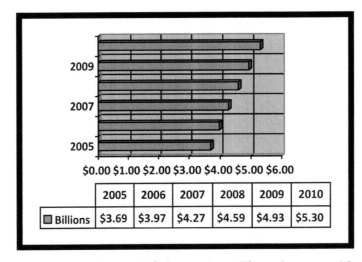

	2005	2006	2007	2008	2009	2010
Billions	$3.69	$3.97	$4.27	$4.59	$4.93	$5.30

Source: Common Sense Advisory, Inc.; *Time*, January 12, 2007

Many companies are not necessarily translation specific but offer things such as international product development, customer support and communications and these businesses are sometimes tied into figures for the translation industry. Many figures also come from businesses that gain revenue from doing interpretation as well as translation.

Inaccurate estimations also stem from the differences between localization and globalization. All organizations and companies are currently dealing with how to communicate to foreign counterparts and they are all potential clients for your new company.

Key Markets

Key markets include: advertising agencies, banks, law offices political firms, offices, courts, Fortune 500 companies, manufacturing companies, government offices, trade associations, non-profit agencies, hospitals/healthcare systems, hotels, food/beverage companies, defense/aerospace plants, consulting firms, insurance companies, debt collectors, cell phone companies, tourist attractions, convention centers, and universities.

Opportunities for items and documents to be translated are endless. Medical & legal documents, informational brochure, websites, and advertising are the largest portion of things that you'll see as translation projects. Companies are always anxious to have their website translated because it gives them the ability to reach clients from all over the world without having to work too hard at it. If any company is serious about taking their company international, they almost always contract someone to do the translation of their website and supporting material.

It is important to know which markets you want to reach and emphasize your strengths in these areas. If your background is law or medical then you would want to consider interpreting or translating in that field. Accurate data is currently being collected by the government so that businesses and individuals will have a better reading and understanding of what the translation industry has to offer. Projections for the translation industry growth are around 20% annually for many companies and businesses.

Interpreters and Translators who know obscure languages or specific dialects within more well-known languages are often able to develop niche markets with their unusual knowledge.

In addition to the translation of documents and the interpretation of the spoken word, many agencies offer related services, including the following:

- Language instruction
- Testing and consulting
- Creative Document design & formatting
- Telephone interpretation
- Trade-show support

- International marketing
- Video and film subtitling
- Software "localization"
- Foreign-language telemarketing

Translation Industry Growth Drivers

There are many things driving the market, here are a few growth drivers

- Growing demand for translation of computer and software manuals into many languages.

- An increasing number of companies entering emerging markets (like China and India), requiring language services to help train workers and create sales and marketing materials to introduce their products.

- Government intelligence and security agencies responding to terrorism concerns and issues related to entry into the U.S. by immigrants.

- The growing diversity of many small American communities, requiring social services agencies to contract with firms to provide language services to new populations.

Source: Wall Street Journal, November 2, 2006; Time

Technology & the Industry

Memory Software
An area of growing importance and assistance in the linguistics industry is the development and constant improvement in the Memory Software Program market. This will be of great aid to translators in the industry. Memory software programs can cut down on a great deal of time and work for translators when they are typing up a translation project. What

the software does is assist in the translation by suggesting words that you've used in other projects.

Being fluent in two languages can be just as confusing as it sounds and many things can get lost in translation. Double checking the accuracy of words and their meanings are imperative but with memory software, you only have to do that once. Obviously it's a good idea to double check things every so often to make sure terminology hasn't changed, but with memory software, you cut down on the never-ending dictionary look-ups, which takes up a majority of your time.

Success Factors

Niche & Value Propositions in obtaining Business for Translators and Interpreters......In business there are commonly 3 things you can be good at- services, price, quality. However, it is almost impossible to be all three, so you must pick 1-2.

Here are a few ideas and areas to focus on to help you stand out from your competitor's:

- Specializing in a particular area/industry. Whether it is law, medical, business or a technical field, it is critical to have an understanding within the areas of business you are providing services.

- Specializing in particular languages. While some of the larger language service providers can offer all things to all people. Most firm owners say they have found more success by offering services in a set number of languages. (ex. Specializing in German & Russian)

- Contracting and outsourcing with experts. Enlisting the help of experts to assist on projects that need layout and design assistance, website professionals to help with inserting translated text into the website environment if you are not familiar with computer code and marketing experts to help you develop a professional image or brand for your company. This is very important as competition enters your market or area. Instead of doing this type of work on your own (and nowhere near as professional or as fast on most occasions), business owners and freelancers should spend their time doing what they do best, providing language services, managing language projects and looking for new business.

- Marketing and advertising continually. Once a few new clients are engaged, some firms stop their marketing and advertising efforts. This can be a costly mistake, because as soon as contracts are fulfilled, if they have not properly executed their business-development plans, a serious "dry spell" can occur in which no projects are schedule.

Phrases & Terms Used in marketing & advertising material that has been used successfully by companies in the language industry:

Years of Experience	**Member, ATA**
Specialty- Asian, Legal, etc.	Certified Interpreters
All Native Speakers	No. of Languages Offered
Accurate/Smooth Translation	"Fortune 100 clients"
Confidentiality Assured	Independent Freelance

Hours/Days Available	**Rush Service**
Invitation to Visit Website	Global Locations (Specified)
Competitive Prices	Free Estimates
Quotations by Email/Fax/Phone	24-Hour Emergency Interpretation
7 Days a Week	Quick Turnaround

Proceed With Caution

Translation Websites & Computer Translation Software

There will be times when you may be tempted to use computer assisted translation software programs & websites to help speed up the translation process only to regret it later. These software programs and websites were designed for small sentences and paragraph translations not for the exact translation of major documents on a large scale. The accuracy of these site ranks very low for projects that are more than a few words in length. For instance, a translation of 300 words (approximately one-page of text) that is only 75%-80% accurate means that every 3rd or 4th word is incorrect.

It will take you longer to figure which word is wrong and why (context, misspelled, tense, etc.) than if you had done the translation without the software or website "assistance" on your own. My advice, stay away from these sites. You will read more about quality, accuracy and translation teams later in this book.

Omitting the Proofreading Process

I have known agencies and freelancers that in an effort to save money and time skip the proofreading process all together. You may get away with this a few times, but your mistakes will eventually show themselves at a time and place you least expect it. *"Work done by night is easily seen by day."*

Hiring Sub-Par Staff & Contractors

Another money saving practice is the hiring of staff or contractors that you usually would not use to keep a larger portion of the profits to yourself. Remember, there's a reason they don't work for you on a daily basis. It can be something as small as the contractor constantly forgets to put accent marks in their translations or that they use the wrong context of the word within their work. Either way, there will be errors that you will have to look for within the project and correct. If you don't and your client or their intended audience finds the errors it could be the last project you ever do for that client or in that market (advertising, courts, etc.) since word of mouth can both make or break a business.

Customer Service

Finally, a common mistake of language industry professionals, especially freelancers, is forgetting to provide their clients with great customer service. Without the client you have no business. Make sure that everyone that works for you and with you (contractors, staff, volunteers, etc.) believes this and provides it…or your competitor will.

Average Rates & Fees

Interpreter Rates

Typical rates for interpreters range from $30 to $100 per hour or more, though rates for people with national security clearance who are willing to work in other countries can be significantly higher. One county government office in California reported having an annual budget of $607,000 for 26 interpreters (or about $23,350 each). The average hourly rate for freelance language interpreters varies depending on where you live, competitors rates, experience and credentials (ex. Certified, Language degree, etc.). If someone requests an interpreter on the same-day or the language is rare you can charge an additional fee or a higher rate. **This topic is discussed in more detail in Ch.13 "What Do You Charge?"**

Translation Rates

Translation services are sometimes billed on a per-page basis or per-word basis though it is more common to pay your contractors and to charge your clients on a per-project basis. A typical project fee to a client is $750 for a technical document, product brochure, or series of advertisements. **This topic is discussed in more detail in Ch. 13 "What Do You Charge?"**

If you are a DeSoto Translations Representative/Licensee and need Up-to-Date Rates and Research Material please visit us at:

www.DESOTOTRANSLATIONS.com

(Sources include The Wall Street Journal, December 7, 2004; The Fresno Bee, October 2, 2004; and Profile America, Inc.)
Note: These tips & statistics were adapted and researched from the following sources: www.desototranslations.com, www. translationdirectory.com & www.translation-services-usa.com, American Translators Association, www.atanet.org Translation Journal, www.accurapid.com/journal Multilingual, www.multilingual.com, www.desototranslations.com

"Before everything else, getting ready is the secret to success."

Henry Ford
Founder, Ford Motors

Chapter 3
TRANSLATION MISTAKES
When Words Get the Best of Us

___

Funny translation mistakes are widespread, but as the President of a national language company I know that mistranslations can result in serious consequences when they occur on academic transcripts, immigration paperwork, legal records or other documents. Translation mistakes can lead to incorrect academic evaluations that could deny a student acceptance into the university they just applied to. They even can delay immigration proceedings for someone applying for a visa.

Accurately conveying the meaning when translating from one language to another is absolutely critical. Depending upon the subject matter, sometimes this can mean sticking closely to the source text and other times it requires a looser translation in order to best deliver the central meaning. A good translator knows this and that understanding and ability can make all the difference between getting your message across the way you intended and having your message misinterpreted.

Translations Bloopers

Here are some bloopers and errors made by computer translation software programs, companies that localized the text but not the image and individuals that just didn't check their work before printing it for the masses:

Funny Translation Mistakes

Commission President Jacques Delors asked in French whether he could address a certain committee. The system had him asking whether he could 'expose himself to the committee.'

Coors Beer Company put its slogan, "Turn It Loose," into Spanish, where it was read as "Suffer from Diarrhea."

The Chevy Nova never sold well in Spanish speaking countries. "No Va" means "It Does Not Go" in Spanish.

Clairol Cosmetics introduced the "Mist Stick", a curling iron, into German only to find out that "mist" is slang for manure. Not too many people had use for the "manure stick".

Scandinavian vacuum manufacturer Electrolux used the following in an American campaign: Nothing sucks like an Electrolux.

In Chinese, the Kentucky Fried Chicken slogan "finger-lickin' good" came out as "eat your fingers off".

When Gerber started selling baby food in Africa, they used the same packaging as in the US, with the beautiful Caucasian baby on the label. Later they learned that in Africa, companies routinely put pictures on the label of what's inside, since most people can't read English.

An American T-shirt maker in Miami printed shirts for the Spanish market which promoted the Pope's visit. Instead of "I saw the Pope" (el Papa), the shirts read "I saw the potato" (la papa).

When Parker Pen marketed a ball-point pen in Mexico, its ads were supposed to have read, "It won't leak in your pocket and embarrass you." Instead, the company thought that the word "embarazar" (to impregnate) meant to embarrass, so the ad read: "It won't leak in your pocket and make you pregnant."

A few years ago in the American Midwest some people decided to show off their new "real" Mexican restaurant named Chi-Chi's to some visiting Californians. Upon seeing the name on the marquee, the Californians started to laugh. When asked why they were laughing, they explained that in Mexico the Spanish phrase "chi-chi's" literally means "titties" or a woman's breasts.

Visit our website for more funny translation mistakes at:
www.DESOTOTRANSLATIONS.com

"*You can't push anyone up the ladder unless he is ready to climb himself.*"

— **Andrew Carnegie**
Entrepreneur & Philanthropist

Chapter 4
TOP REASONS TO ENTER THE MARKET
Why Bother?

Why even start up a business? Why continue reading this book at all? Here are several reasons that will light the fire underneath you to keep you motivated and moving forward. One key fact is there is extensive opportunity and growth in this field over the next 25-50 years. According to the most recent census data, a new Immigrant enters the U.S. every 19 seconds. Additionally, Hispanics are the largest ethnic minority group in the U.S., projected to surpass all other ethnic and racial groups by 2050. Spanish translation & interpreting projects make up the majority of work for most U.S. language companies.

If you do not speak English upon arrival to the United States (or the language of whatever country you are entering) there are barriers to resources and support services to help you out as you work towards acculturation and independence. Without the assistance of an interpreter or document translation communication between those in need would not take place. Imagine making money doing something you love to do that could also help people and get paid well for doing it.

Additional Reasons

1. **Prove everyone wrong.** This is your chance. This is your shot. You have the opportunity to show everyone what you're made of. Following your dream just became your reality and you have the ability to do whatever you please with your new venture. There are very few satisfactions in life that can equate to knowing that you were victorious. This is true in sports, gambling, the debate team; you name it. Knowing that you proposed a business idea and were successful is a very powerful thing. All businesses start from a single idea, no matter how farfetched, you have the potential to blossom into the next big thing.

2. **Unlimited income potential.** Money doesn't buy you happiness. We've all heard it. However, imagine if all of the things you never thought possible

for yourself or your family can be a reality with your endless earning potential. You can be as big or as modest as you please. Take competitors, industry, target markets and its potential, into consideration; you can maneuver those things through proven strategies so that the cards are stacked in your favor. The end result is you making a much greater amount per hour than you could if you worked for someone else.

3. **Having your own direction.** Don't feel like coming in today? That's fine! Don't make a habit of it or you will run into problems with your number two reason for starting up. When you start your own business you are your own boss. How many times have you wished you could be your own boss and didn't have someone hovering over you? Now you can be. You can plan your own schedule. Admitting now that when you first start up you may be putting in 16 hour days 7 days a week. But you can reward yourself for your hard work down the road. You also get the ability to be creative and go in different directions with your company as well. I took mine from a small home based business, practically to the moon and back because I had the potential to.

4. **Other reasons**

- Having fun doing what you really like doing
- Possibly working from home
- Networking with like-minded, motivated people
- Creating new employment in your community
- Having influence in your community/the world
- Creating company policies with your values and morals
- Using failure & mistakes as reasons to progress
- Building excellent "comeback" skills
- Having true passion and exuberance for life
- Developing business savvy
- Becoming an expert in your field
- Developing leadership skills
- Setting the pace, being a trendsetter
- Becoming a role model/inspiration for others
- Leaving a legacy for future generations
- Attracting investors that rally to your success
- Using your Native Language and Culture to make a living
- Capitalizing on a business idea

The reasons are endless...

"The journey of a thousand miles starts with the first mile."

— Chinese Proverb

Chapter 5
IN THE BEGINNING

Should I Incorporate?

"For many people, it's the start that ultimately stops them." When you are starting a business it's not always going to go exactly as you planned it. This book will hopefully make the bumpy road a little smoother for you as you get going. There are some initial things you should know when starting out like how to make a good first impression and how to develop a successful business plan. And let's not forget you've got to get an office set up at some point. We will show you how to get by on a shoestring budget, how to go all out if you've got some start-up capital from a rich relative and everything in between.

The start-up process for any business is very difficult. The bumps are inevitable so be prepared to make mistakes and know what you can do to fix that problem so that it doesn't happen again. Your education does not come for free. It is all about learning from your mistakes and using them to grow, remember all it takes in the U.S. to start a business is to say, "I think I'll start a business today," and just like that you are in business. Since you can start your business as easily as saying it (sole proprietor) or by applying to incorporate through a lawyer (incorporation) I wanted to explain the pros and cons of each.

I initially started my business as a sole proprietorship (discussed below) but soon found myself receiving large checks from my clients that I knew would eventually impact my personal income taxes. I visited my local Small Business Administration (SBA) office for advice, the information and contacts I received have been priceless.

One of the key things I remember being told during a workshop was; *"Get a good lawyer and a good C.P.A. (Certified Public Accountant), these two individuals will help make and keep your company's profits."* I actually met the lawyer that would later incorporate my business and draft one of my company's first and most profitable agreements to-date as well as my accountant at the SBA office.

One company with several names (DBA's)

Just before I officially incorporated my CPA sat down and showed me that there were two structures that could work for me but in the long run I would personally be suited with one over the other based on our companies 5 year growth plan which was to get bigger. I had several businesses and initially thought I would need to incorporate each. If there is no financial or legal reason for a separate corporation for each business you can simply file a *Doing Business As (DBA) Form* at your local city or county office for a minimal cost (average fee is $15 to $50).

You can now use different names for your business and projects or use a revised name for marketing purposes instead of the name used for the incorporation documents. This will also save you money when you file your annual taxes since you will use the same tax I.D. number for the various DBA's and file one tax return. *(Ex. Johnson Construction, Inc. DBA Johnson Concrete Services, Inc. or DBA Johnson Residential Services, Inc.)* You will need to file a separate DBA Form for each separate or different business name.

No matter which business structure you decide on, since this is a highly technical area, and you will probably require further information based on the amount of revenue and other personal and financial details specific to your situation. It is recommended that you consult a competent professional such as a qualified tax accountant, C.P.A. or attorney. Several of the more established tax and legal professionals will provide an initial 1-hr consultation for free.

Don't feel obligated to sign on as a client if you do not feel the advice or personal style of the consultant or firm are to your expectations. There have been many occasions where the rep, lawyer or agent that was trying to get my business was just too pushy or too relaxed. If I didn't feel that a long term relationship was possible I simply thanked (and paid if necessary) them for their services and moved on. Even if you have to pay a fee for some of the advice or initial financial or legal services you receive, do not look at it as a cost, consider it an investment that will provide you with a return at a later date.

Corporation Structure Types

There are several types of corporation structures, I am going to highlight the 5 most Basic Types of Corporation Structures. Again, if you'd like more information I would advise you meet with a lawyer to discuss the differences and which would be most beneficial to you considering your specific goals and objectives.

Sole Proprietorship

Sole proprietorship is the easiest type of entity to form. You don't even need to fill out any paperwork in most states to call yourself a sole proprietor. "Sole proprietor" essentially means a person does business in his or her own name and there is only one owner. However, this entity legally has no separate existence from its owner. All debts of the business are debts of the owner. It is a "sole" proprietor in the sense that the owner has no partners. A sole proprietorship is not a corporation; it does not pay corporate taxes, but rather the person who organized the business pays personal income taxes on the profits made, making accounting much simpler. A sole proprietorship need not worry about double taxation like a corporate entity would have to.

A sole proprietor may do business with a trade name other than his or her legal name. However, in some jurisdictions, for example the United States, the sole proprietor is required to register the trade name or "Doing Business As" DBA name with a government agency. This also allows the proprietor to open a business account with banking institutions using the DBA name.

Corporations

Anyone who operates a business, alone or with others, may incorporate. This is also true for anyone or any group engaged in religious, civil, non-profit or charitable endeavors. You do not have to be a business giant to be able to have the financial and other benefits of operating a corporation. Given the right circumstances, the owner(s) of a business of any size can benefit from incorporating.

General Corporation

This is the most common corporate structure. The corporation is a separate legal entity that is owned by stockholders. A general corporation may have an unlimited number of stockholders that, due to the separate legal nature of the corporation, are protected from the creditors of the business. A stockholder's personal liability is usually limited to the amount of investment in the corporation and no more.

Advantages

1. Owners' personal assets are protected from business debt and liability.

2. Corporations have unlimited life extending beyond the illness or death of the owners.

3. Tax free benefits such as insurance, travel, and retirement plan deductions.

4. Transfer of ownership facilitated by sale of stock.

Disadvantages

1. More expensive to form than proprietorship or partnerships.

2. More legal formality.

3. More state and federal rules and regulations.

Close Corporation (or C Type Corporation)

There are a few minor, but significant, differences between general corporations and close corporations. In most states where they are recognized, close corporations are limited to 30 to 50 stockholders. In addition, many close corporation statutes require that the directors of a close corporation must first offer the shares to existing stockholders before selling to new shareholders. This type of corporation is particularly well suited for a group of individuals who will own the corporation with some members actively involved in the management and other members only involved on a limited or indirect level.

S Corporation (or S Type Corporation)

With the Tax Reform Act of 1986, the S Corporation became a highly desirable entity for corporate tax purposes. An S Corporation is not really a different type of corporation. It is a special tax designation applied for and granted by the IRS to corporations that have already been formed. Many entrepreneurs and small business owners are partial to the S Corporation because it combines many of the advantages of a sole proprietorship, partnership and the corporate forms of business structure. S Corporations have the same basic advantages and disadvantages of general or close corporation with the added benefit of the S Corporation special tax provisions. When a standard corporation (general, close or professional) makes a profit, it pays a federal corporate income tax on the profit. If the company declares a dividend, the shareholders must report the dividend as personal income and pay more taxes.

S Corporations avoid this "double taxation" (once at the corporate level and again at the personal level) because all income or loss is reported only once on the personal tax returns of the shareholders. However, like standard corporations (and unlike some partnerships), the S Corporation shareholders are exempt from personal liability for business debt.

S Corporation Restrictions

To elect S Corporation status, your corporation must meet specific guidelines. As a result of the 1996 Tax Law, which became effective January 1, 1997, many of these qualifying guidelines have been changed. For more detailed information about these changes and other aspects regarding S Corporation status, contact your accountant, attorney or local IRS office.

Limited Liability Company (LLC)

LLCs have long been a traditional form of business structure in Europe and Latin America. LLCs were first introduced in the United States by the state of Wyoming in 1977 and authorized for pass- through taxation (similar to partnerships and S Corporations) by the IRS in 1988. With the recent inclusion of Hawaii, all 50 states and Washington, D.C. have now adopted some form of LLC legislation for both domestic and foreign (out of state) limited liability companies.

Many business professionals believe LLCs present a superior alternative to corporations and partnerships because LLCs combine many of the advantages of both. With an LLC, the owners can have the corporate liability protection for their personal assets from business debt as well as the tax advantages of partnerships or S Corporations. It is similar to an S Corporation without the IRS' restrictions.

Advantages

1. Protection of personal assets from business debt.

2. Profits/losses pass through to personal income tax returns of the owners.

3. Great flexibility in management and organization of the business.

4. LLCs do not have the ownership restrictions of S Corporations making them. Ideal business structures for foreign investors.

Disadvantages

1. LLCs often have a limited life (not to exceed 30 years in many states). Some states require at least 2 members to form an LLC, and LLCs are not corporations and therefore do not have stock -- and the benefits of stock ownership and sales.

As with the S Corporation listing, these lists are not inclusive. For more detailed information, please be sure to speak with a qualified legal and/or financial advisor.

How You Can Benefit from a Corporation or LLC

Regardless of their size, most businesses can benefit from incorporating. Advantages of forming a corporation or Limited Liability Company (LLC) include:

Personal Asset Protection

Both corporations and LLCs allow owners to separate and protect their personal assets. In a properly structured and managed company, owners should have *limited liability* for business debts and obligations.

Additional Credibility

Adding "Inc." or "LLC" after your business name can add instant authority or credibility that a sole proprietor does not have. Consumers, vendors, and partners may prefer to do business with an incorporated company.

Name Protection

In most states, other businesses may not file your exact corporate or LLC name in the same state.

Perpetual Existence

Corporations and LLCs continue to exist, even if ownership or management changes. Sole proprietorships and partnerships just end if an owner dies or leaves the business.

Tax Flexibility

Though profit and loss typically *pass through* an LLC and get reported on the personal income tax returns of owners, an LLC can also elect to be taxed as a corporation. Likewise, a corporation can avoid *double taxation* of corporate profits and dividends by electing Subchapter S tax status.

Deductible Expenses

Both corporations and LLCs may deduct normal business expenses, like salaries, before they allocate income to owners.

Should I Incorporate or Form an LLC?

Corporations and LLCs are both separate legal entities (business structures) that enjoy certain protections under the law and important benefits. Most people form a legal business structure to safeguard their personal assets.

Incorporating, or forming a Limited Liability Company (LLC) allows you to conduct your business without worrying that you might lose your home, car, or personal savings because of a business liability.

Because a Sole Proprietor is the easiest type of structure to form most people starting out in the language industry begin their business as a sole proprietor, then as business picks up they incorporate shortly thereafter.

For more detailed information, please be sure to speak with a qualified legal and/or financial advisor. If you are a DeSoto Representative and/or Licensee you can visit www.DESOTOTRANSLATIONS.COM to incorporate or file your Doing Business As (DBA) application forms.

"Did you ever notice that when you put the words "The" and "IRS" together, it spells "THEIRS?"

—Unknown

Chapter 6
OTHER LEGAL STUFF
Certifications, Tax I.D. and other Credentials

Business & Sales Licenses

Before putting your "Open for Business" sign up, you may want to take a step back and make sure you've covered any additional bases. There are certain licenses and permits that are required and they vary from place to place. You may have state, county, and city rules and regulations to follow before opening up shop so be sure to check into each area before you get too ahead of yourself. Luckily, because most language translation and interpreting businesses are Service Based with no inventory, sales tax and sales licenses are more than likely not necessary.

First off, is there a business license needed in your town or state? Each city has a business licensing department that serves as a tax-collecting bureau and does not act as any public service at all. In most cities you will simply have to pay a fee in order to operate you business in that city. Some towns and cities however, will make you give them a percentage of your gross sales each year. It's most common in small cities that a portion of your annual sales will go to them in the form of a tax.

There will be a difference depending on where you are located — some places require a county permit if you are outside of city limits. State and federal licenses may be in order as well depending on your state. It's usually uncommon in the translation industry, but check with your state to be on the safe side.

Minority & Women-Owned Business Enterprises

There may be a license you could get that will actually be in your advantage such as one through the Minority and Business Enterprise or the Women in Business Enterprise. Some of the benefits are getting an equal opportunity at some of the state's contracts, you also get considered for subcontracting bids where the main vendor needs to give a portion of the work to a certain percentage of women owned and minority owned business each year and being affiliated with the MBE or the WBE will give you an automatic in.

Zoning Ordinances

If you plan on running your company out of your house and you want to make it legitimate, look into what the zoning ordinances are in the area that you live in. Some neighborhoods do not allow businesses. Go to your local office for zoning — it will probably be located within your city/county offices. Make sure you have all of the questions you need answered written down ahead of time so that you only have to make one trip and you get everything answered that you need to move forward.

Signage

Putting up the sign for your business is not as simple as picking out the design and making sure it's level. Many cities and areas have sign ordinances about the location, size, and lighting of your sign as well. Renters will also have to go through the landlord to see if they have any stipulations about putting up a sign. When I was leasing a building everything from the colors I used in my sign to the hours it could be lit were an issue. Just make sure you cover all of your bases before you start putting up signs all over the place that will need to be taken down because you didn't get permission.

Tax ID & DUNS Number

If you incorporate you'll need a federal tax ID number obviously for federal tax purposes. To set that up you'll need to contact your nearest Local IRS Field Office or go online. My lawyer applied for a Tax I.D. when he filed my incorporation papers. The form you will need to fill out is an IRS SS-4 form, or if it's just you running the business and you have no other employees the IRS will want you to label the top of your form "For Identification Purposes Only." This helps them out and probably saves you work in the long run.

It is a good idea that you also get a DUNS number, which stands for Data Universal Number Service, for your company. A DUNS number is an identification number that you receive through the government for your business which makes it credible within the marketplace. It is usually used and most necessary within the Wall Street and Stock Market area. This number also makes you easily identifiable to other businesses and companies and makes it easier for customers to locate your business and learn about the services you offer. Most companies require a DUNS number if you are going to do business or have a contract with the U.S. government or several Fortune 500 companies.

A DUNS number will also act as a way of performing background checks on your company for loans and other things. A DUNS number is free to request and all you have to do is go online and register for one. It takes about 5 days to get one online or you can call and get your number in a single day.

NAICS Code

Along with a DUNS number you will need a North American Industry Classification System code, or a NAICS code and it is used to measure economic activity in Canada, Mexico, and the United States. You can search for the codes on the census bureau website.

The NAICS Code for the Language Interpreting and Translation industry is: NAICS CODE: 5419300- Translation & Interpretation Svcs

This code is requested by several government offices, the IRS when you file your taxes and companies that plan on bidding on government contracts. Additionally, several court contracts will ask for this code when you submit your invoices after you interpret or translate for government institutions (federal court, prisons, etc.).

Insurance (Errors & Omissions E&O Insurance)

It is standard for professionals and agencies in the languages industry to purchase Errors and Omissions (E&O) Insurance to protect them in case of a lawsuit. This type of liability insurance protects you and/or your company from claims if your client holds you responsible for errors, or the failure of your work to perform as promised in your contract. Talk with your insurance agent regarding your options. They should have referral and recommendation information since many standard insurance agents (Life, Auto & Home) do not carry this type of coverage. The cost annually can vary from a few hundred dollars to a few thousand dollars for a large language agency.

If you are using contractors you can choose from contractors that have this type of coverage as an incentive for the contractors to get the coverage and to protect all parties from this type of liability.

Check with your local SBA office or Chamber of Commerce to see if there are any additional forms, licenses or permits needed to conduct business in your area.

"Education is when you read the fine print. Experience is what you get if you don't."

— **Pete Seeger**
American Folksinger & Activist

Chapter 7
CERTIFICATION
Are You a Certified Interpreter/Translator?

One of the questions I get asked all the time is "is certification mandatory if you want to be an interpreter?" Although it is not a law, some states and government agencies will only use interpreters and translators that have received some type of documented training or certification outlining their skills and abilities as an interpreter.

Documenting your credentials, qualifications and ability as an interpreter and/or translator will be one of the best, yet most time consuming things to accomplish. When I started my company I hired interpreters using internal standards and tests created in-house. However, over the years there have been several companies, universities with special degree programs, hospitals and government organizations that have developed assessments, programs, trainings, tests and certification programs to document your ability as an interpreter from one language to another and that you understand the "language," etiquette and procedures used in specific industries (ex. Courts, Hospitals, Engineering, etc.).

Be sure to research the certification program you are interested in since some can be cost prohibitive, time intensive and industry specific (ex. Court Certification, Medical Certification, etc.). Also, because most certification programs are new they may be limited on the languages available and testing dates as well as space to sign-up for programs. Currently, Spanish court and medical certification programs are the most common certification programs available in the U.S..

Recently, there have been innovations in on-line certification and degree programs allowing individuals seeking certification to do so from the comfort of their home and as their schedule permits. There is an extensive resource list at the back of this book. Also, visit the website www.desototranslations.com for more up-to-date information as well as certification website links.

Court Interpreter Program Overview

What is a court interpreter?

Spoken language court interpreters interpret in civil or criminal court proceedings (e.g., arraignments, motions, pretrial conferences, preliminary hearings, depositions, trials) for witnesses or defendants who speak or understand little or no English. American Sign Language interpreters interpret for all parties who are deaf or hard of hearing in all proceedings.

Court interpreters must accurately interpret for individuals with a high level of education and an extensive vocabulary, as well as for persons with very limited language skills without changing the language register of the speaker. Interpreters are sometimes responsible for translating written documents, often of a legal nature, from English into the target language and from the target language into English.

What do court interpreters do?

Court interpreters have an important job in the courtroom: they interpret court proceedings for witnesses and defendants with limited English skills or for parties who are deaf or hard of hearing. The position requires strong memory and communication skills. Court interpreters shift between two different languages, in real time, accounting for different types of speech and grammar. They also know legal terms and commonly used courtroom forms and reports.

Are court interpreters in demand?

Very much so, according to a recent study, more than 200 languages are spoken in California alone. Of the state's 36 million people, about 20 percent speak English less than "very well." That's almost 7 million Californians who would need help from an interpreter if they found themselves in court.

What does it take to become a court interpreter?

First, interpreters need to be fluent in both English and a second language. Listed below are 13 of the most common languages available for court certification:

American Sign Language
Arabic
Armenian (Eastern)
Armenian (Western)
Cantonese
Japanese
Korean

Mandarin
Portuguese
Russian
Spanish
Tagalog
Vietnamese

People who master other languages can become registered interpreters with the same full-time pay and benefits that certified interpreters receive. However, they may need to submit a letter of recommendation from a past client or professor listing their credentials and experience. It is at the client's discretion whether or not this is acceptable documentation to be considered equivalent to an actual certification program or test.

Court Interpreters

Interpret speech and text from English into a second language and back again in real time. The interpretation must be accurate without any editing, summarizing, omissions, or change in meaning. Maintain good working relationships with judges, attorneys, other court personnel, supervisors, and coworkers. They also need to understand a variety of court procedures and practices.

Is special training recommended to become a court interpreter?

Yes. Court interpreting is a very demanding job. Spoken language court interpreters must be completely fluent in both English and the second language, while court interpreters of American Sign Language must be completely fluent in both English and American Sign Language. The level of expertise required for this profession is far greater than that required for everyday bilingual conversations and general interpreting. The interpreter must be able to handle the widest range of language terms that may be presented in the courts—from specialized legal and technical terminology to street slang. Most people do not have a full command of all registers of both English and the foreign language and, therefore, require special training to acquire it.

Although there are no minimum requirements that must be met in order to apply to take the most certification tests, applicants are encouraged to complete formal, college-level course work and training in both languages and modes of interpreting before applying for the examination. At present there are several colleges and universities throughout the United States that offer introductory courses and certificate programs in interpretation or translation.

However, as I pointed out earlier, most of these are for English/Spanish. We encourage you to contact the schools and/or organizations providing the certification you are interested in and request information about their programs.

For the other languages, the following self-study techniques are suggested:

1. Expand your vocabulary

2. Develop your own glossaries

3. Develop interpreting techniques

4. Keep a list of clients you have provided services for

Suggested skills-enhancing exercises are available to help you develop three interpreting techniques:

1. Consecutive interpretation

2. Simultaneous interpretation

3. Sight translation

Why should I become certified?

Certification is a way to document that you possess skills and knowledge that allow you to perform effectively in the interpretive profession.

Is certification required to work in the field?

Not at the moment. Certainly, many talented people who are not certified work in various areas of providing interpretive services. What certification does is recognize that you have the basic skills and knowledge required to assure quality interpretive services.

Will certification help me get a job or higher pay

I can't promise that. However, it won't hurt. Keep in mind, your employer may or may not recognize certification as proof of your abilities or as the basis for a promotion or raise in pay.

What does it cost?

The cost to become a certified interpreter can vary depending upon the certifying organization, length of program, and materials needed to prepare and/or take the certification test. I have seen costs as low as $25 to take a one-day course at a hospital and as high as $10,000 to take a semester long course that eventually ended with the individual taking the certification test. Also, if the certification program you are signing up for is from an accredited college or university and you hope to get a degree in interpreting or translation you could pay thousands more than the costs mentioned above.

Additional costs that need to be taken into account:

1. Unless you live in a big city plan on spending money for hotels, food & travel since most tests will be offered in a bigger city or neighboring state.

2. Study Guides if they are not included in your registration fees

3. Loss of income for the times you are away or studying for certification

How long does it take?

This will depend on the type, language and organization providing the certification. I have seen online programs that can be completed in a few minutes, programs that take a few hours, 1-day programs, 1-week programs, programs with several dates over a number of months (Orientation on the first month, Verbal Test a few months later, Written Test a few months after that, etc.) and programs that you can only take if you meet certain standards (Ex. college student in specific degree program)

Are there levels of certification?

Depending on the type, language and organization providing the certification there may be varying levels of certification and expertise (Expert, Basic, General, etc.). Also, some programs, degrees and certifying institutions may have more credibility or familiarity than others.

*Warning

I have personally come across programs and tests that are intentionally designed for the person not to pass on the first or even second time so that the "testing" organization can make money on additional materials and services (ex. Study guides, reference books, re-testing fees, etc.). There are several government agencies that have outsourced their testing to private companies will little to no oversight. Be sure to ask what methods and standards will be used to assess your credentials, certification and final test score.

You may find that subjective and personal preference in wording and/or terminology may be what's keeping you from successfully passing your certification exam. Biased and subjective testing has no place in interpreter certification testing, but I see it happen quite often. If you feel that you have been the victim of biased or subjective testing bring it to the attention of the testing organization or the company that contracted the testing company.

On the other hand, there are some programs that will pass anybody that pays the testing fee. Be sure to research the certification program you wish to pursue before signing up to begin.

There is an extensive resource list at the back of this book. Also, visit the website www.desototranslations.com for more up-to-date information as well as certification website links.

*"Always do right-
this will gratify some and
astonish the rest."*

— Mark Twain
American Author & Humorist

Chapter 8
ETHICS & THE LANGAUGE INDUSTRY

Did I Do the Right Thing?

What is ethics? When is something ethical or unethical? According to Webster's New World Dictionary the word Ethical is defined as: 1. Having to do with ethics or morality, 2. Conforming to moral standards and 3. Conforming to the standards of conduct of a given profession or group.

Whether you will be providing the services yourself or contracting others to perform the work, it is vital that you familiarize yourself with the ethics, rules, norms and standards for individuals and companies involved in language services and the GILT Industry. Below are examples of codes of ethics used in some courts and health systems. When you apply to become certified or to work for a language company you will most likely sign a confidentiality agreement as well as code of ethics policy that you agree to adhere to.

This chapter includes examples of confidentiality and ethics policies you will encounter in the language industry.

The Medical Interpreters Code of Ethics

Confidentiality
Interpreters must treat all information learned during the interpretation as confidential, divulging nothing without the full approval of the client and his/her provider.

Accuracy: Conveying the Content and Spirit of What is Said
Interpreters must transmit the message in a thorough and faithful manner, giving consideration to linguistic variations in both languages and conveying the tone and spirit

of the original message. A word-for-word interpretation may not convey the intended idea. The interpreter must determine the relevant concept and say it in language that is readily understandable and culturally appropriate to the listener. In addition, the interpreter will make every effort to assure that the client has understood questions, instructions and other information transmitted by the service provider.

Completeness: Conveying Everything that is Said

Interpreter must interpret everything that is said by all people in the interaction, without omitting, adding, condensing or changing anything. If the content to be interpreted might be perceived as offensive, insensitive or otherwise harmful to the dignity and well-being of the patient, the interpreter should advise the health professional of this before interpreting.

Conveying Cultural Frameworks

Interpreters shall explain cultural differences or practices to heath care providers and clients when appropriate.

Non-Judgmental Attitude about the Content to be Interpreted

An interpreter's function is to facilitate communication. Interpreters are not responsible for what is said by anyone for whom they are interpreting. Even if the interpreter disagrees with what is said, thinks it is wrong, a lie or even immoral, the interpreter must suspend judgment, make no comment, and interpret everything accurately.

Client Self-Determination

The interpreter may be asked by the client for his or her opinion. When this happens, the interpreter may provide or restate information that will assist the client in making his or her own decision. However, the interpreter will not influence the opinion of patients or clients by telling them what action to take.

Attitude toward Clients

The interpreter should strive to develop a relationship of trust and respect at all times with the client by adopting a caring, attentive, yet discreet and impartial attitude toward the patient, toward his or her questions, concerns and needs.

The interpreter shall treat each patient equally with dignity and respect regardless of race, color, gender, religion, nationality, political persuasion or life-style choice.

Acceptance of Assignments

If the level of complexity or personal beliefs makes it difficult to abide by any of the above conditions, the interpreter shall decline or withdraw from the assignment.

Interpreter should disclose any real or perceived conflict of interest that could affect their objectivity. For example, interpreter should refrain from providing services to family members or close personal friends except in emergencies. In personal relationships, it is difficult to remain unbiased or non-judgmental.

In emergency situations, interpreters may be asked to do interpretations for which they are not qualified. The interpreter may consent only as long as all parties understand the limitations and no other interpreter is available.

Compensation

The fee agreed upon by the agency and the interpreter is the only compensation that the interpreter may accept. Interpreters will not accept additional money, considerations or favors for services reimbursed by the contracting agency. Interpreter will not use the agency's time, facilities, equipment or supplies for private gain, nor will they use their positions to secure privileges or exemptions.

Self-Evaluation

Interpreters shall represent their certifications(s), training and experience accurately and completely.

Ethical Violations

Interpreters shall withdraw immediately from encounters that they perceive to be in violation of the Code of Ethics.

Professionalism

Interpreters shall be punctual, prepared and dressed in an appropriate manner. The trained interpreter is a professional who maintains professional behavior at all times while assisting clients and who seeks to further this or her knowledge and skills through continuing studies and training.

Professional Ethics and the role of the court interpreter

The guidelines provided here are intended to help you deal with difficulties that frequently arise in the courtroom. It is important to remember, however, that the judge is the final arbiter of what is appropriate in their courtroom, and ultimately you must defer to the judge. There are also many unwritten rules in every courtroom, and you as an interpreter have a duty to learn and obey them as well.

Accurate Interpretation

A court interpreter's best skills and judgment should be used to interpret accurately without embellishing, omitting, or editing.

At the beginning of any legal proceeding, the interpreter takes an oath swearing to "well and truly interpret" that proceeding, or words to that effect. The court interpreter actually has a twofold duty: 1) to ensure that the official record of the proceedings in English reflects precisely what was stated by a non-English-speaking witness or defendant in another language, and 2) to place non-English-speaking participants in legal proceedings on an equal footing with those who understand English.

It is important to remember that the judge and/or jury will be relying entirely on the interpreted version of testimony to draw conclusions about the credibility of the non-English speaking party and non-English-speaking witnesses and the relative weight of testimony. Therefore, you must convey every single element of information that was contained in the original message, in a close to a verbatim form as English style, syntax, and grammar will allow. By the same token, the non-English-speaking witness should hear precisely the question that was asked, without simplification, clarification, or omission.

Register: You must never alter the register, or language level, of the source language message (the language from which you are interpreting) when rendering it into the target language (the language into which you are interpreting) for the purpose of enhancing understanding or avoiding offense. For instance, if the attorney asks, "What did you observe the subject to do subsequently?" you should not say in the target language, "What did you see him do next?" You should not try to bring the answer down to the witness' level, nor should you intervene and say you don't think the question is understandable to the witness.

If the witness does not understand the question, he should say so; it is not the interpreter's job to speak up for him.

It is important to remember, when interpreting a witness' testimony before a jury, that the jury will draw certain conclusions regarding the witness' sophistication and intelligence, based on his or her work choice, style, tone, ect. It is your job to make sure the jurors have as much information in that regard as a native speaker of the target language would have in order to judge the witness' credibility.

Word Choice: Nuances of meaning are critical in courtroom testimony. One study found that subtle changes in word choice significantly altered witness's recollections of events. When a key word in the question was changed ("About how fast were the cars going when they hit/smashed/collided/bumped/contacted each other?"), subjects who were asked the question that contained the term "smashed" tended to increase their estimate of the speed, and recalled seeing broken glass when in fact there was none. Thus, you must be very careful in selection target language terms to make sure that they accurately and precisely reflect that source language meaning.

Idioms and Metaphors: Idioms are phrases that have meaning which is not merely the sum of the words contained in them. Examples of English idioms are "you're welcome," "to run the gamut," and "so much the better." Metaphors are descriptive expressions that portray one situation in terms of another, such as "he tore his hair out trying to solve the problem," or "she was caught red-handed." You must always try to find an equivalent idiom or metaphor in the target language; do not translate them literally. Remember that the primary focus in interpreting is conveying meaning, not translating individual words.

Obscenities: If a witness uses foul language or says something that might be damaging to his or her case, you should not edit out the offending terms; interpret exactly what you hear, conserving the original meaning. Remember that the jurors will make judgments about the honesty and credibility of this witness on the basis of his or her manner of testifying. They should not be at a disadvantage because they do not know the target language. For cultural reasons, obscenities are particularly difficult to translate directly; a word-for-word translation may be meaningless in the target language. You should look for the closest equivalent in the target language, striving to elicit the same reaction from target language listeners as the original message would elicit from source language listeners.

Repetition: Repetition and redundancy are important factors in evaluating witness testimony. You should not add or subtract any words for the sake of clarity or expediency. Thus, if a witness says in the source language, "I, I, I didn't see it," you must say exactly that in English, not simply, "I didn't see it." Redundancies should also be preserved in the target language version. For example, when an attorney says, "Did you watch and observe him at all times?" you should not omit the redundant verb in the target language version.

Self-Corrections: Many speaker, attorneys and witnesses alike, make false-starts and then revise their statements. It is especially important in interpreted witness testimony that all such self-corrections be included in the target language version, so that they judge and jury can draw conclusions about how certain the witnesses about is or her testimony, or how precise he or she is in choosing his or her words. Never correct any errors made by a speaker, no matter how unintentional they may be.

Third-Person References: It is common for people who use interpreters to preface their statements with phrases like "Tell him that…"and "Ask him if…"rather than addressing each other directly. If they do so, you must not edit out those phrases. If someone repeatedly makes third-person statements, ask the judge to instruct them on the proper procedure.

Embellishments, Clarifications, Editing: It is important never to add anything or elaborate on the message you are interpreting, not even for the sake of clarifying or smoothing over choppy delivery. The interpreter's function is not to make people sound more articulate or logical in the target language than they did in the source language. If a witness gives a response that is inappropriate to the courtroom setting, such as "uh-huh" instead of "yes," you should refrain from converting the answer to more appropriate language.

Fragmentary Statements: Courtroom testimony does not always proceed logically, as if following a script. Witnesses often speak unclearly because they have told their stories many times before and assume that everyone knows what they are talking about (e.g. "I went to the…you know… and there was…it was there." Such vague and ambiguous statements are difficult to translate to another language, because more information is needed to choose the proper pronouns, prepositions, and verbs. If they are brief and vague you will be as well, without inserting any additional information to clarify the statement.

Nonsensical Testimony: It is particularly difficult to interpret the testimony of a person who is highly excited or has mental problems and does not necessarily make sense. It is important for the interpreter to make every effort to state exactly what the witness said, no matter how illogical or irrelevant it may be. Sometimes this is very difficult because of ambiguities or incomplete phrases uttered by the witness; in such cases, you should inform the court that you need to clarify the witness' statement before proceeding to interpret it. But under no circumstances should you edit, omit, or add to what the witness stated.

Emotions: Triers of fact (juries) need to have a clear understanding of the emotions such as anger, fear, shame, or excitement that are expressed by witnesses. Humans convey their emotions not only in words, but also in facial expressions, posture, tone of voice, and other manifestations. These non-linguistic means of expression are very closely tied to culture and language, so when people don't speak the same language they may misunderstand the emotional content of a message. The court interpreter has an obligation to convey emotions in a way that seems natural in the target language, rather than merely repeating words like an automaton. Thus when an aggressive attorney is bearing down on a witness to try to intimidate him or her, you should be equally forceful. And when the witness answers questions in a timid way, you have to convey the emotions expressed by the witness in a slightly attenuated form. If you were to burst into tears or scram out loud exactly as the witness did, it would make a mockery of the judicial process. If a witness expresses emotions in such an overt way (and the manifestations of these emotions are the same in the source language and target language cultures) the judge and jury can observe the witness's behavior and draw their own conclusions for that; there is no need to mimic the witness.

Interpreter's Emotions: It is imperative that you keep your own emotions in check; the only emotional reactions you should express are those of the witness you are interpreting for. This may be very difficult at times, such as when graphic photographs of crime scenes are shown to witnesses, when a witness unintentionally says something funny, or when a witness is clearly lying. Nonetheless, you should strive at all times to reflect only the reactions of the parties you are interpreting for. The jury should b judging the credibility of the witness, not that of the interpreter.

Hand Gestures: Pointing or gesturing is another important element of communication. If you try to reproduce a gesture that a witness makes, there is a danger that you might mischaracterize his or her testimony (pointing to a slightly different part of the body, for example, or making a gesture that has a different meaning in the target language culture). If a witness includes a gesture in his or her testimony, refrain from reproducing it; simply interpret the witness' words (e.g. "He hit me here."). The judge and jury can see the witness themselves, and it is up to the attorney to describe any physical movement made by the witness so that the transcript will accurately reflect it.

Conservation or Clarification of Ambiguities: Anyone who has studied language knows that words change meaning as their context changes. Sometimes the meaning of a word is ambiguous because the listener does not have enough contextual information. The English pronoun "you," for example, can be either singular or plural, and the speaker may not clearly indicate which meaning he or she has in mind. Moreover, some terms may require more information to be translated from English into another language. For example, the word "cousin" could refer to either a make or a female; in many languages, that kinship term is gender-specific rather than generic. As an interpreter, you must clarify any ambiguities before interpreting a message.

Ambiguities may be intentional, however, and you should strive to retain them if the target language allows. It may be possible, for example, to interpret the question "Where did the car hit you?" into the target language without clarifying whether the questioner is referring to the location of the accident or the part of the witness's body. On the other hand, attorneys will often ask this deliberately ambiguous question: "Did you have anything to drink in the car?" or "Was there anything to drink in the car?"

If you cannot retain the ambiguity in the target language but the context makes it clear which meaning is intended, you should clarify it in your rendition. But if you are not certain of the meaning or are aware that the ambiguity is deliberate, you must inform the court that you cannot render the target language version without first clearing up the doubt. It is not the interpreter's job, however, to correct the attorneys' questions. If a question is vague or compound, the witness' answer will be ambiguous, but the problem is the same whether the language is English or any other. Since the problem is not language-related, therefore, you should not interfere. It is the duty of opposing counsel to object to the question; if there is no objection, go ahead and interpret the question.

Both, language company owners as well as their staff and contractors should be familiar with these practices, policies and procedures.

Source: Model Code of Professional Responsibility for Interpreters developed by the National Center for State Courts. The California Judicial Council for Interpreted Proceedings and the Code of Professional Responsibility that governs interpreters in the Federal Courts and DeSoto Translations Code of Ethics.

"A good plan today is better than a perfect plan tomorrow."

— Proverbs

Chapter 9
BUSINESS PLAN BASICS

Failing to Plan is Planning to Fail

When I first started my company I was not a big fan of plans, I did a lot of things by the seat of my pants and was very successful, so I thought. One day as I was talking to a friend who was also in business , we began discussing my recent financial success and I stated that my company had made close to a million dollars that year and had a huge profit as well. He asked two simple questions; "Is that what you planned to accomplish?" Secondly, "How do you know that you couldn't have made more?" Without a plan or roadmap to compare and gauge the success of my business, I had no idea. Someone once said to me, *"You can get anywhere in business if you don't have a map or a destination."*

Nowadays I am a big advocate of planning, preferring to error on the side of overplanning on some occasions. One of the first things to do as you prepare to enter any project is to have a basic plan of attack or in this case a business plan. Keep in mind that this is simply a guide and can be revised and updated as often as needed. If you can't put the basics of your plan down on 1-2 sheets of paper you are over thinking the problem. Most investors want a 1-page business plan summary and a 1-page financial overview of what it will cost to accomplish your plan successfully. Once you have a basic "1-pager" plan then you can move on to the prettier and more detailed business plan to use with banks, investors and advisors.

The business plan forces you to have a realistic outlook for your company and to look at all aspects of the business before you jump into the project blindly. Simply mapping things out in your own head is not enough for this part of the start-up. The business plan allows you to view your business from every angle both as an insider and an outsider so that you will know every aspect before you begin the big push of starting your new operation.

The finished product provides you with a basis for your entire company. There are several software packages on the market as well as companies you can hire for a nominal fee to help you write the business plan as well as free services in business planning and assistance from your local Small Business Administration (SBA) office. Once completed the business plan can act as a proposal for partners, clients, and applying for potential loans. Remember, Keep It Simple Stupid (K.I.S.S.).

Business Plan Basics

A strong business plan, no matter what the company is, includes specific aspects of the company and attempts never to leave someone questioning.

Business Plan 101

Cover Sheet- Simple enough right?

Title Page- Still not a difficult task. The hardest part you will encounter will be word usage and trying to make everything sound just as you want it.

Statement of purpose and summary- A preview of what is to come in your business plan/proposal.

Table of Contents- A simple layout will do just fine

Description of business- Explains exactly the service that you will be providing, and why you expect to be able to sell your service profitably or more efficiently.

Market analysis and strategy- Includes financial statements that project the income and expenses for your business for at least three-five years.

SWOT Analysis- This showcases your strengths, weaknesses, opportunities, and threats to your development. Think of it as a job interview, when you state your weaknesses you don't want to make them too weak. Be honest and optimistic but still remain positive and realistic.

Management Structure- Acknowledges the experience that you or other members of your team possess (ex. You, key interpreters or staff members, etc.)

Time tables and schedules- Come up with an outline for when you plan to accomplish things by. This will keep you on task if you know that you've set a goal or deadline.

Financial data- Provides an explanation of the funding that will be needed to operate the business and your expected sources of such funding.

Support System- Identifies any professional advisors that you will be using including an accountant, lawyer, tax advisor, banker, and insurance agent.

Summary- Wrap it all up in a nice little bow with an ending summary that reiterates your general plan and why you intend to be successful in this new venture.

Entrepreneur Magazine, SBA, and Commerce Department websites have examples you can download for free.

Website Resources:

Entrepreneur Magazine: www.entrepreneur.com

SBA: www.sba.gov

Commerce Department: www.commerce.gov

"Before borrowing money from a friend, decide which you need more."

— Unknown

Chapter 10
MONEY MAKES THE WORLD GO ROUND
How to Get Start-Up Money & Manage It

There are a few essentials to establishing an office. You can easily work from home or open your own office, either way you will need a workspace. There are some specific things that you'll need for either and some bare minimum things you will need to run the office.

As the owner it is important to know exactly what services you will offer so that you have all the necessary equipment to meet those requirements.

"Find a good accountant and an even better lawyer. One will help you keep the money you make; the other will protect it all."

Starting your own business **IS** an investment. You will have to put time as well as money into your idea to get it going. I have actually met people that have asked me to invest in their idea or business and when I asked them how much they were putting in, they replied Zero, because it was too risky. If you don't believe enough in your idea/business to put your time and money in the project no one else will invest in it.

There are also those who believe that it has to be all or none. Meaning, they have grand dreams with modest pocket books which is why they can't start or accomplish their idea. "If I could just get 5 million I could start my business the right way. If I can't get the 5 million there is no way it will start or even succeed." Or the ultimate perfectionist that will not settle for their idea to start small then grow because that is not how they planned it. Life is crazy and S!@# happens. You need to be flexible, sensible, persistent and follow your dreams wherever they may take you or you will never be able to get your project going and most important, completed. The most successful people in business are those that understood and adopted this belief and when things didn't go their way or the 5 million dollars in venture capital for expansion became $500 dollars from their personal savings account and kept moving forward. An old friend and very successful businessman told me a story one day as I was having a miserable time on the golf course.

This story stuck with me, he said, *"Business and golf are a lot alike. As long as you keep things moving forward and make progress you will get to where you want to be. Whether it's an inch or a yard, the most important thing is to keep making progress. Occasionally you will run into a few sand traps and there will be times when you will have to go back a few yards so that you can make progress, but if it is the smartest thing to do so that you can continue to move forward that is what you do. Stay focused on the task at hand. Focus on the goal of the game. Keep making progress. And remember, it's only a game, enjoy yourself."*

Since that day I have become so much more relaxed in both my golf game and business. This has lead to me making smarter decisions in both as well as my personal life. I'm sure there are similar stories and metaphors that you have heard or come across that you have adopted and I applaud you. I encourage you to search for your motto if you have not found the maxim that you live by yet. It did help a little that it came from someone I respected and had already had great success in his business career.

Start-Up Money

When it comes to getting money around to start your company you have a few options. You knew it wouldn't be free right? Remember that there is a less expensive and a more expensive way to do things. Regardless though you'll need some amount of capital to work with for start up costs and other things outlined in the budget section of this book. You can work from a lender, your own pocket, friends and family, gaining a partner, or many other options. If you are taking your business along the less expensive route you may only be looking at $500 to $1,000 of a personal investment. I don't want anyone to go bankrupt following their dream so you may have to keep that job you hate or at least not quit till the business is generating revenue and some profits.

I do not encourage quitting your day job or putting all the pressure on your partner or spouse to provide. Do not put all your eggs in one basket unless you are certain you can fail and still be okay. You need to know that it could take as little as 30 to 90 days or as long as 1 to 3 years or longer before you start seeing substantial profits and/or a return on your investment. This is definitely something to consider when making your decision to enter the linguistics industry and when talking with possible investors.

How big or small you go will depend on how quickly you make your money back or the *Return On your Investment (ROI).* If you invest $500 to get started and you get a $500 project off the bat, then you are back on your feet. I would never advise someone to take a financial risk they couldn't afford, only a calculated risk that they believed they could achieve. You know your capital situation better than anyone so evaluate your ability and see what you are willing to potentially invest with little to no return before you begin. Look into creating a business plan to get your money back. If you can't survive without the $10,000 you invested then don't invest your own $10,000.

If you decide to go the more expensive route you'll need to find money from somewhere, couch cushions (although it's never turned out to be very profitable for me), your bank account, or lenders. The important thing is to know what you are getting into. Plan ahead of time so that you know what kind of debt you are willing to take on as well as the terms for people who want to invest. Even if you can afford to go all out and spend major capital to get started you may want to reconsider if you have no managing experience. It doesn't pay off in the end to go big if you have no idea what you're doing. You can always expand if you find you are doing well, but it's much more difficult to cut back on things when you have loans to pay back or you have spent so much at the beginning of the business that you have nothing to invest later when you really need it.

I would first suggest talking with a financial planner or a CPA. It can cost anywhere from $100 to $300 dollars, but in the long run it's better than potentially losing your house.

Money Sources

Savings

I would first suggest financing your operation yourself if you can afford it. If you truly believe in your company you should be willing to put your own money into it. Also this way you won't have any interest to pay back on a loan. Be sure to talk everything over with your spouse or partner before you put anything up that is also theirs as well.

Personal Loans

Taking out a personal loan is a good idea towards getting your start up money. Putting your name behind something will make you want to work harder since it's you on the line and it seems more like your money. If you feel comfortable doing so you can use your house or your car as collateral. But like I said, I don't want anyone losing anything, only put up what you are willing to potentially lose if things take a turn for the worse.

Cash out 401K

You may have a slight fee to pay for cashing out your 401K but it could be a source of capital to start your business. You'll typically pay a fee originally determined when setting up the account for early termination.

Credit Cards

Taking out credit cards in your company name is a great way to gain credit for your business and an easy solution to getting things for start up now and paying later. Just don't go too crazy. Building your credit is great, but not if you can't pay things off and are eventually going to ruin it in the long run. Only purchase things on credit cards that you know you'll be able to pay off in the near future. Don't forget that late payments and missed payments will affect your credit, in this economy business owners need all the good credit they can get.

Line of Credit

A line of credit can be issued to you by banks or other businesses. They are usually short term and allow you to borrow set amounts of money to be paid back at a quicker pace. The main point of a line of credit is to help your company with cash flow.

Amounts of $10,000 to $25,000 on average can be borrowed without you having to put up any collateral and interest rates vary. It's good to have in case of an emergency if something comes up and it's better to have one and not use it, then to not have one and be stuck in a pinch.

You will often get offered loans you don't need especially if you have good credit. But don't get too ahead of yourself. All of that credit is often seen as just debt that you have and when you need something big like a new vehicle or home, it's going to be that much harder to obtain those loans if banks see you have too much debt. Remember if everything you sign-up for in your company is in your name, and potentially your spouse's name they can also be held liable for everything you invest in, which can be really good, or really bad.

You may be tempted to go the "Cadillac" route, but don't let your head get too big. If you want a huge office that's fine, but it will cost more and your customers may begin to think they're paying for your office as well as your services. I also do not advise anyone to waste resources that could be used more wisely.

The 3 F's- Friends, Fools, and Family

This is your group of people to turn to in a time of need; those who either feel obligated to help you out, or are easily coaxed into the deal. The key thing to remember is that you should keep this very professional. Have a lawyer draw up papers and contracts on the terms and conditions of the loans. Be honest with them and remember that it may take 1 to 3 years for your company to turn *really* profitable. Don't burn any bridges with those close to you and make sure you keep the investment strictly professional.

Small Business Administration

SBA loans are like the tooth fairy. You aren't sure if it exists, sometimes here and there you may see proof or hear of someone getting a loan but those instances are few and far between. But it's worth a shot. I would suggest applying for one and seeing where it gets you but don't rely on getting anything back.

Partners

Taking on a partner with your business is a judgment call you will have to make all on your own. It may seem great in the beginning if they are willing to help you invest and provide start up funds, but keep in mind they will obviously want something in return. Commonly they'll ask for around 20% of annual profits or maybe it would be a partnership where you both do everything 50/50. It may be less work or debt for you, but keep in mind it will also mean less profit and control. Most investors are also in it for the money and they want to make their return as fast as possible, usually within 3-5 years.

So if something is good in the long run of the project but will not add to the value of the project right now or its selling price it probably won't happen. Think of the project like a house that you and your partner are trying to flip for a profit. You might want to live in it eventually, but your partner just wants to sell it for as much as possible as fast as possible. You think hardwood floors would look great but it costs twice as much and will take twice as long to install than carpet. You better believe that those floors will be carpeted. Now that you have a partner you will have to do what is best for all parties involved, which will definitely lead to disagreements along the way if you and your partner do not see eye to eye.

Venture Capital

This is a type of private capital usually provided by professional, outside investors to new, high-potential-growth companies in the interest of taking the company to the next level. Venture capital investments are generally made as cash in exchange for shares in the invested company. A venture capitalist (VC) is a person who makes such investments and a venture capital fund is a group investment vehicle that primarily invests the financial capital of third-party investors in business operations that are too risky for the standard loans.

Most venture capital comes from a group of wealthy investors, investment banks and other financial institutions that gather the investments. The downside is that venture capitalists usually get a say in company decisions, in addition to a portion of the equity. If your investors do not buy into your vision or direction you could eventually be at odds with one another, as part owners they could out vote you in certain key decisions. Worst case scenario, you could be voted out as CEO and relegated to just an owner.

Networking

Some ways to cut cost are by networking instead of traditional marketing. It is something that you should engage in regardless, but when you network you are your own billboard, you are your own commercial. Go ahead and honk your own horn if you need to in order to make sure your business is out there and known.

Mentors

You shouldn't have to go at it alone. It's always good to know someone who knows about business and can offer you advice when you come to bumps in the road. A mentor is priceless because the time and money they save you as well as the connections you will make from the people they will introduce you to could never be calculated. Go to someone who is successful in *their* industry, it doesn't have to be translation at all, just someone who is thriving in their business or industry.

The networking opportunities and people you'll meet through your mentor are endless, not to mention the experience they'll offer you. I would suggest someone with 20 or more years of experience. Don't burn any bridges and ruin the relationship by asking them for favors or handouts. People are more willing to do favors for friends, so if you are on a friend basis rather than strictly professional acquaintances it's okay to ask for a favor from time to time. I usually take my mentors to dinner every few months. Keep in touch but don't bombard them with simple questions or go to them for every single problem you have. They are busy people so use your time with them very wisely.

Another type of mentor you may have is someone that you have a personal relationship with. Someone that will keep you motivated and on track is always good to have around. You will get some great stuff just bouncing ideas off of each other.

Cash Flow

A banker once asked me during a loan application interview if I was having "Cash Flow" problems, I replied, *"No. I was having problems getting people to pay me on time and for that reason I was getting behind on paying others."* This, my friends, is the essence of "cash flow."

SIX STRATEGIES FOR MANAGING CASH FLOW

Keep your overhead as low as possible. A majority of overhead is salary and contractors, and the rest is maintenance, running the business and marketing. Keep your expenses as low as possible, even during flush periods.

Keep two to four months of overhead in a savings account for rainy days. Not only will it be important for practical reasons, it also will give you peace of mind. Don't touch that money unless you really have to. Tapping into that account should be a red flag that the business is not generating enough cash flow to cover your expenses. It could be your billing, your marketing or your flow of prospects. That's the time to find out what's wrong and fix it.

Open a business line of credit. It's like having a business credit card that you draw money against, but it's a large amount of debt as well, usually $25,000 or more. It generally costs $100-$200 a year to keep this type of account open, but it's worth it because it will be there in case you need extra funds to cover yourself for a couple of months.

Become a merchant and take credit cards for payment on jobs. You pay a small percentage per transaction for the convenience (which you can also bill to the client), but the benefits outweigh the tiny cost. It puts money in your pocket right away. You do the job, and you get paid the same week. And you'd be surprised how many clients will appreciate being able to use their credit cards, including corporate clients with corporate credit cards. They like it because they usually get benefits, such as frequent flyer mileage points.

Negotiate with your vendors. As you develop strong relationships with your vendors you can negotiate better payment terms. Why would they give you better terms? Because you are loyal to them and you give them a lot of business. Instead of the usual thirty days, ask for sixty or ninety days. Every little bit helps. Then, when you do pay them, use a credit card, which gives you another thirty days.

Put deposits in escrow. In order to avoid a situation whereby you get paid upfront and then spend the money before the actual bills come in, put that money in a escrow account so you don't spend it, and so it can earn interest until you have to pay the vendor. Check with your bank to get more details.

Bookkeeping and Tracking Expenses

There are tools you can use to facilitate this process. QuickBooks and PeachTree are two popular accounting software programs for small business that allow you track your expenses and bill your clients. These programs may appear to be complicated to a creative mind like yours, but they're not. They just take some time and instruction if you are going to do it yourself. It's well worth the investment of time to learn QuickBooks, whether you teach yourself or hire a bookkeeper to get you set up.

Once you have all the information in place and up to date, you can create any kind of report you need any time of day. You can look at your profit and loss, your bank balance, what you're spending with a certain vendor, how much a particular client has been worth year to year, and which clients are more than thirty days late in their payment so you can make a few collection calls instead of being hit with a cash flow crunch down the road.

If you don't have the time or the knowledge to invest in this essential aspect of your business, don't let it go. Hire a bookkeeper to come in and do it for you for three or four hours a week. It's a perfect solution for a small business. The bookkeeper does data entry, payroll, bill-paying and reconciling the bank statements. He can even do your billing for you.

Raising Your Rates

Raise your rates

Every year or two, language service firms begin thinking about their pricing, and specifically whether to raise it and how to go about it. Here are a few thoughts for you to consider.

How to Raise Your Rates

First, don't think of your hourly rate as a pricing tool, because it's really more of a positioning tool. It is just one of many inputs that feed how prospects and clients view your services, but it is substantive one. How much you charge per hour is directly related to the perceived value of your services. In fact, the only time you should talk about your hourly rate is when you want to make a positioning statement or in answer to a direct question asked by a prospect or client. Otherwise, don't talk about it. Talk about value.

Second, don't think of your hourly rate as a way to make money, because making money is more about utilization than pricing. To expand on this, there is absolutely no correlation between a firm's hourly rate and how much money they make, but there is a very direct correlation between how many hours they get paid for versus how many hours they spend on any given body of work.

The latter distinction is about utilization, or what we call "billable efficiency." If a given firm is not making enough money, they often are tempted first to raise their hourly rate, but that's going straight to second base without first rounding first base. First base is making sure that you're capturing all your time properly, no matter at what hourly rate you're capturing all your time properly, no matter at what hourly rate you're billing it. Keep this issue separate, and fix your utilization first. If you've fixed that and still want to make more money, or if your current hourly rate is too low from a positioning standpoint, then think about raising your hourly rate.

Third, concentrate on being consultative rather than getting trapped in a transactional mentality. Using hourly rates for interpreting appointments makes sense but it makes no sense when dealing with translation projects.

Translation projects require a particular, focused expertise, which in turn allows for a process of solving client problems that is defined and proprietary. As a consultant people will look to you to solve the problem using various methods and systems allowing you to charge a more reflective rate for the services you are providing. Having embraced these points, suppose you want to adjust your hourly rate? Here are some suggestions on how to do it.

6 Strategies For Raising Your Rates

First, don't change it every year. Doing so is transactional, as if the rate of inflation is built into your hourly rate. It is not, and thinking that way will make you look more like a seller of commodities than of advisory/consultant of services. So look at it every year, but change it every three to five years.

Second, change it by a significant amount or don't bother (assuming that you don't have a lot of catching up to do in the first place). That means you'll increase it typically by ten to thirty dollars per hour (10%-30%), or it's not worth the disruption.

Third, if that disruption would endanger some of your client relationship, just do it for prospects (i.e., new clients). There's only so much compromise that's prudent when trying to keep "legacy" clients happy, but sometimes it's a short-term solution you're willing to entertain as you bite your tongue and live with it until you have better choices. Remember, you will have client turnover, if it's for the right reasons let it happen. I have dropped clients that didn't want to pay rate increases, at some point in time they either need to pay a rate increase (even if it is not the full increase) or you need to let the client go.

Fourth, tell those who need to know a couple of months in advance, and then say no more about it when the time comes.

Fifth, position the price increase as an inevitable outcome from a careful look at your profitability targets. In other words, do an internal study that leads to (surprising) findings that virtually requires you to raise your rates to meet those targets. Make it a considered move and not some gut reaction, and then blame the study that you wish you could argue with but cannot.

Sixth, try to provide choices to individual clients. Above all, that's what clients want. Even choosing between two bad options gives them the sense of control, which every client craves. There is no question about raising your rates, but the net effect to clients can be minimized by giving them options such as doing less work for them, having them give you the necessary materials and information farther in advance and accepting fewer rounds of changes.

Finally, remember that this is never as big of a deal as you anticipate. The fear builds in your head, but you'll almost always be surprised at how much of a non-issue this is to clients if handled appropriately. Your best clients want you to make money and appreciate what you do, that's why they send you work.

Rules for Donating Services and Pro-Bono work

Nonprofit does not mean "no profit." Nonprofits are still running a business; it's just that at the end of the year, when they close their books, if there is a profit, it ideally goes back into the services they provide instead of being distributed among shareholders or owners.

Nonprofit does not always mean they're looking for pro bono, either. A healthy nonprofit will budget for marketing and design like any other business. In fact, some nonprofits have big marketing budgets because they know the value of marketing. It's a line item in their budget-and that includes contracting interpreters, professional services to cover the costs of translation services and layout.

Smaller nonprofits ($2 million or less operating budget), however, of which there are hundreds of thousands all over the country, are usually looking for pro bono work. If you want to work with nonprofits, it's better for your business to look for bigger nonprofits that have marketing budgets to work with.

Here are some guidelines to follow to follow if you want to work with nonprofits or do pro bono work:

- Believe in the cause. You must have a passion for the cause. With the large number of requests you will receive for pro bono work, you need to realize you will need to create some personal guidelines in regard to denoted time. Consider donating your services if the project is related to education, cultural issues, nonprofit groups, children's causes or issues in which you have a strong personal interest. Only take on a limited number or percentage of pro bono projects in any one calendar year.

- Make it a fair exchange. Pro bono work is not "free" work. You're giving something of value to the organization, and you are getting something in return. You may be doing it for a warm, fuzzy feeling. You may be doing it for exposure. Whatever your reason, be clear about it because, unfortunately, the IRS does not recognize work that is done pro bono, so there is no tax benefit. The IRS states: "Although you cannot deduct the value of your time or services, you can deduct the expenses you incur while donating your services to a qualified organization." So make sure to track any out-of-pocket expenses so that you can deduct them later.

- Maintain your quality standards process. Don't let your standards process fall by the wayside just because no money is changing hands. Your contract will be even more important in this type of situation. As you would with any other client, adhere to your schedule and the acceptable number of revisions, updates and time spent on the project.

- Make sure they have a budget to produce what you translate. You don't want to find out in the middle of the process that they only have $500 to translate the annual report you translated. That's a waste of your time and resources. Bring this up in the early stages of the process and, if you find out they don't have enough of a production budget, offer different options for translation.

- Ask for creative latitude. One of the reasons to do pro bono work is to create work for your portfolio, so be sure to negotiate for the opportunity to use more creative flexibility in the project.

- Will you get paid if the work is not used? What if the event or project for which you're translating material for is canceled at the last minute? Does your work simply disappear, and are your efforts for naught? Be sure to stipulate in your contract what happens if the work is not used, whether it be a payment to you or something else.

- Present your work to the board of directors. One good reason to do pro bono work is for exposure and connections with people in important places. Before you agree to anything, negotiate to present your work, perhaps in its final form, to the board of directors of the nonprofit. In fact, you should insist on this. These boards often are made up of civic-minded business people who travel in very different business and social circles from you. And they are generally very good net workers. It's essential that you meet them in person (rather than be offered the chance to follow up with them later) to make that personal connection.

- Get a translation credit. Negotiate for an actual credit on the work, whether it's printed or electronic. In both cases, a web address is the best credit you can get because it not only tells the name of your firm; it also directs new prospects to your web site, where they can learn more about your services.

- Ask for samples. One main reason to do pro bono work is to be able to show it off, which you can't do unless you have plenty of samples. So ask for at least a hundred samples, and then use them in your promotional efforts.

You can easily do a separately targeted mailing built around this one piece at very little marketing expense.

- Get mentioned in their press release. Often, a nonprofit will take advantage of free publicity and will send out a press released to the project, especially if it's a high-end job for an event or activity. Ask to be included in the media coverage. All you need is one or two lines to describe your involvement, which, when posted online, will be good for your search engine rankings as well.

- Set boundaries. Know when it's done. These projects can go on forever, especially when there are no payment terms. Be strict about what you give and what they get. It will protect you in the end.

- These rules can also apply to working with family and friends.

Remember to keep the process as professional as possible in order to avoid potential miscommunication or unrealistic expectations.

Should I Barter or Trade?

Although it's less popular, bartering can be an acceptable alternative for a cash-starved client offering an exciting creative opportunity. Check with your accountant, because barter arrangements may be taxable. When bartering, make sure you negotiate, in writing, an equal value exchange. For pro bono and nonprofit work or for projects you accept at a reduced rate, you also can ask for full creative control and compensation for all out-of-pocket expenses.

The downside is that you risk establishing a reputation for these types of arrangements, possibly lessening the perceived value of your services. If you decide to negotiate such nontraditional agreements, treat them like your other professional relationships and have them approved, in writing, by the client. Also, always emphasize that you're proposing a nontraditional, one-time agreement that may not to be applicable for the next project.

Now that you have clarified your own policies about the way you handle money in your business, make sure you talk about these policies with your clients.

"Excuse me, I believe you have my stapler."

— Milton Waddams
Office Space

Chapter 11
EQUIPMENT, SUPPLIES & SOFTWARE
....What Program Is This File In Anyway?

Tools of the Trade

Compared to other businesses starting a service based company has a very low-cost advantage because of the minimal amount of equipment and supplies needed especially in starting a language translation and/or interpreting business. Another advantage of a service business is that there's no inventory.

Desktop Computers

It's obvious; you know that you need a computer. In this industry and practically in any industry these days it is impossible that someone will not need a computer. There are several different types, models and designs. Some come pre-loaded with software and some come without any. At the very least you will need a computer with lots of memory to accomplish the tasks you will need it to perform as well as an operating system. A computer with an Operating system like Windows XP or Windows Vista as well as anti-virus software is basic.

I had no idea what that meant when I went to get a computer, but if you go into a store that carries computers and electronics they can point you in the right direction as to which computer to purchase with the basic amount of hardware, memory and proper operating system. I would advise you get the best computer you can afford with the most memory you can afford, it will be a wise investment.

Laptop Computers

A laptop or desktop will be a choice you make based off of what fits your lifestyle best. If you think you'll be traveling a lot or working from outside the office then maybe a laptop is the right choice for you. Generally desktops can be cheaper but keep in mind the amount of memory required. Whichever you choose, try not to go too inexpensive and keep in mind all of your work will be on this one computer. If you opt to go the cheap route, you could lose more in the long run if you lose all of your projects on a bad computer when, not if, it crashes.

This can cost you more overall than you paid in the beginning with repair fees or potentially buying another computer. I encourage you to purchase the most inclusive (usually the most expensive) service and support plan you can afford. It is not a question of if, but a question of when will your computer get a virus, breakdown or die all together. Although we wish they would work forever, your computer will from time to time need to be repaired and eventually replaced. Will it be sooner or later?

Additional Software and Hardware

Computer Software

Microsoft software programs like Microsoft Office are the most popular software programs in the world. It is important to use programs common to both your industry and clients so that you can share information across platforms.

Design Software

Adobe Creative Suite 4 or higher (which includes Photoshop & PageMaker, etc.) so that you can receive projects from your clients in the original programs the content was created in for the purpose of conducting word counts and inserting the translated text once the project in completed. If you do not have design software or someone that is familiar with how to navigate them then you will need the software below.

Saving/Sharing Files Software

Adobe Acrobat Pro 9.0 or higher. This software will allow you to create, save and make changes to Pdf's.

Translation Memory Manager Software

Translation memory software, or TM, is a database that stores segments that have been previously translated. A translation-memory system stores the words, phrases and paragraphs that have already been translated and aid human translators. The translation memory stores the source text and its corresponding translation in language pairs called "translation units".

Some software programs that use translation memories are known as translation memory managers (TMM). Translation memories are typically used in conjunction with a dedicated computer assisted translation (CAT) tool, word processing program, terminology management systems, multilingual dictionary, or even raw machine translation output.

Research indicates that many companies producing multilingual documentation are using translation memory systems. In a survey of language professionals in 2006, 82.5 % out of 874 replies confirmed the use of a TM.

Examples of Translation Memory Manager Software

Here is a list of 4 of the common software programs available:

1. SDL Trados
2. Déjà vu
3. WordFast
4. AnyMem

Word Count Software & Websites

You will need to conduct a word count of almost all translation projects. These are some software programs and websites that will help you get an accurate word count regardless of the type of program it was created in: CAT Count, WordCountTool, AnyCount and ClipCount.

External Hard drive/Memory Drive

You will need at least 1 Gig of external memory to save projects. I encourage you to save projects daily at the very least. You can find this minimum memory capacity in most memory thumb drives/memory sticks and maximum capacity in external memory towers capable of saving several computer hard drives. There is also online memory websites that you can store all your files to, which also makes backups of all your files every few hours, for a reasonable fee. Companies include Carbonite and Xdrive.

Printer

You will need a good quality printer with color printing for your client's projects that you print out and so you can make high-quality presentation materials. If you are doing large amounts of copying (2000-5000 copies) monthly, a good way to save money is to lease a copier that can accommodate this volume. If you are not doing a large amount of copies you are better off buying a less expensive printer ($100-$300) and buying ink as needed.

Internet

If you are going to avoid getting a fax machine it is even more important to have internet connection with e-mail. This will be a main way of getting in touch with clients and the necessary way of getting the projects to you via e-mail. This also eliminates the step of retyping the projects if you translate them directly on the computer. It will save you time and money as well.

I personally like to have as fast of an internet connection as I can afford so the quicker the internet connection the quicker you can get your work done. Most projects will be large and simple dial up won't be enough to open large files or graphic design projects for translating. I would suggest high speed internet but remember, buy only what you can afford.

Phone with answering/message system

If you're not getting a cell phone then you absolutely must have a land line or home phone so your clients can get in touch with you and leave messages when you're unavailable. Have an answering machine so that when you are not home or in your office people can still leave you messages. It is also a smart idea to have call waiting so you never miss an important call. One missed call could be one missed project. If you file a DBA or incorporate with the state it will qualify you to get a business listing and number in the phonebook. This could be very beneficial since a lot of people use whitepages.com, yellowbook.com and the actual phone book when they are looking for assistance and service providers in their area.

Answering Service

An answering service is a call center that answers the phones for you as if it were one of your employees (ex. *Good afternoon, this is Jane with Company X, How may I help you?*) when you are not in and takes all of your messages when you are not available. Shop around and look into prices because this may overall be a cheaper option. This will also help in presenting your business in a professional manner and give the perception that your company is larger than it actually might be initially. Try and meet with them and let them know exactly what you are looking for in a call center so they know what is expected of them.

Cell phone

You will need to have some way for people to reach you if you are working out of a home office. It is good to have a cell phone with you so that people can reach you at all times, if you plan on being out a lot and are conducting 24-hr interpreting or translation services. Depending on how much you will use your phone you will know what plan works best for you. A pay as you go non-contract may work best if you don't think you will need very many minutes. As always be careful when signing any contract. If you go on a one or two year plan with a contract make sure you know what you are getting in to and be cautious of hidden fees that will show up on your monthly statements.

PDA/Smart Phones

A Personal Digital Assistant (PDA) or Smartphone is a mobile phone offering advanced capabilities, often with PC-like functionality. There is no industry standard definition of a Smartphone. For some, a Smartphone is a phone that runs complete operating system software providing a standardized interface and platform for application developers. For others, a Smartphone is simply a phone with advanced features like e-mail, Internet, synchronized calendar capabilities and/or a built-in full keyboard or external USB keyboard. In other words, it is a miniature computer that has phone capability. Phones like the iPhone, Blackberry and Palm Treo are making it almost redundant to have both a phone and a computer when your phone can do everything and more than your computer.

Work Space

Working from home requires a separate work space for all of your business work. Even if it's as simple as a table in the room or a separate room set up as an office. Having a separate place to work will allow you some peace and quiet to get things done and also keep you on track and most importantly, organized.

Leasing Space

If you will be leasing an office be sure to read the terms of lease thoroughly, there are several ways that a landlord can slip in fees or terms in their favor or that are simply not standard because they can tell you're new to leasing office space. It is better to start off small and eventually get more office space or move to a larger location. Most entrepreneurs do the opposite however, they get more space than they need and have a hard time filling it as well as paying for it. Even if you've got money to burn, getting office space that is bigger than you need, expensive and sensational may come back to haunt you one day.

I personally had a landlord lease me office space in an area that was on the edge of the business district for nearly 3 times what they were charging other tenants in the same building and for a mandatory 3 years, terms no other tenant were subject to. Although *"Predatory Leasing"* is not a crime it does happen a lot more than you think.

After leaving the office I just mentioned I leased a different office and although the lease and terms were considerably better than the previous lease, the lease had a huge "grey area" in it when it came to what constituted "repairs" and what constituted "maintenance" issues. The landlord was responsible for all repairs and the tenant (me) was responsible for all maintenance. What I realized was that in the landlords' eyes unless the piece of equipment in question (heater, air conditioner, electrical system, etc.) exploded, it was not a repair issue, but a maintenance issue that I would have to pay for. Since this building was a bit older things were constantly breaking.

Dictionaries/Resource Books

If you are doing your own translations and not outsourcing projects, make sure that you have an accurate dictionary for each language that you will be translating, such as English to French/French to English dictionaries.

Staples and Fed Ex Account

Having a Fed Ex or Staples business account can cut down on your time and save you money with discounts and rewards. Both businesses will have your company information stored so you can just drop things off to be shipped or pay for things quickly. Staples will have your business information so that you get billed for your supplies at a later date.

Business Cards

Business cards are maybe the most important thing. This is a way for people to get in contact with you that you meet in the community. Be sure to include all contact information as well as your business hours (ex. 24-hr, 8 a.m.-5 p.m., etc.) If you are just getting a cell phone, be sure to have that on your card. If you are working from home and don't feel comfortable with people sending information to your home office you can get a P.O. Box.

Remember to put what you do on the card as well. I have seen some great cards that have all of the contact information on them and they look great, but it never states what the person does. If you will be translating yourself put "translator," or if you will be outsourcing your translations then "language consultant" would be best to put on your business card.

Letterhead & Envelopes

When you are sending out letters to other businesses and companies, it looks a lot more professional to have a letterhead designed to send information out on. To save money you can design your cards, letterhead and envelopes yourself in WORD, PageMaker or Photoshop which all come with predesigned templates.

Additional items for your office

- Furniture

- Office Decorations

- File Cabinets

- Book Shelves

- Office Supplies

See the budget samples in the next chapter for additional items and start-up costs.

"Some couples go over their budgets very carefully every month; others just go over them."

— **Sally Poplin**
Author

Chapter 12
BUDGETS
Things Always Cost More Than We Plan

Budgeting lies at the foundation of every business plan and financial plan. It doesn't matter if your business is floating paycheck to paycheck or bringing in six-figures a year, you need to know where your money is going if you want to have a handle on your finances. Unlike what you might believe, budgeting isn't all about restricting what you spend money on and cutting out all the fun in your life and it's not as hard as you may think.

It's really all about understanding how much money you have, where it goes, and then planning how to best allocate those funds. Here's everything you need to help you create and maintain a budget for you and your business.

Budgeting Basics

Do you know why a budget is so important? On the surface it seems like creating a budget is just a tedious financial exercise, especially if you feel your business finances are already in good order or because you are the sole employee you don't need one. But you might be surprised at just how valuable a budget can be. A good budget can help keep your spending on track and even uncover some hidden cash flow problems that might free up even more money to put toward your other financial goals.

How to Create a Budget

The hardest part of creating a budget is sitting down and actually creating one. It's like staring at a blank piece of paper when you need to write something and that first step seems like a massive hurdle. Don't worry--I've broken down the budget creation process into a few easy to follow steps. You'll be able to sit down and create a basic business budget in just a few minutes.

3 Traits for Budgeting Success

Once you've taken the time to create a budget, now it's time to make sure you follow it. Budgeting can be like going on a diet—you start with good intentions, but after a few weeks or months you drift away from your plan. Don't let that happen to you. Here are a few basic traits that will ensure budgeting success.

1. Basic Budget Worksheet

If you're having difficulty coming up with all of the various expense categories for your budget, I've created a budget worksheet that can help you organize everything. This worksheet has the most common expenses and can help you keep track of everything in an orderly fashion.

2. How Overspending Breaks Your Budget

The main reason to create a budget is to help you keep your finances under control by keeping track of how much money you're spending and where it goes. When you begin to stray from your budget it's usually because of spending too much money somewhere. But if you have a budget that tells you exactly how much you're supposed to spend, why is it so easy to overspend? There are a number of reasons we overspend, so when you understand what causes overspending, you can help put a stop to it and keep your budget on track.

3. Try Using Cash to Keep Spending Under Control

Swiping plastic has become incredibly easy. With both credit cards and debit cards, we can be in and out with a purchase in a matter of seconds. Unfortunately, this convenience comes at a cost. By using plastic we can begin to lose track of how much money is actually being spent. Sure, two dollars here, 4 dollars there, it doesn't seem like much at the time of purchase, but if you aren't careful they can really add up and bust your budget. One trick to help keep your daily spending under control is to use cash instead of your credit or debit cards. It might not be as fast, but it helps you visualize just how much money you're actually spending.

Costs	Low Annual Estimate	High Annual Estimate	1-Time Costs Start-Up
Advertising	$3,000.00	$24,000.00	$5,000.00
Bank Charges	$300.00	$2,000.00	$50.00
Bookkeeping services	$3,000.00	$15,000.00	
Cell phone	$1,200.00	$3,000.00	$300.00
Conference/Training Registration	$1,000.00	$2,500.00	
Contractors 28-30% (Interpreters, Proofreaders, Translators)	$1,000.00	$75,000.00	$1,000.00
Dues (Membership/Association)	$100.00	$2,500.00	$500.00
Electric	$2,400.00	$5,000.00	$250.00
Equipment purchase (Phone system, fax, visa machine)	$5,000.00	$50,000.00	$15,000.00
Errors & Omissions Insurance	$180.00	$3,000.00	$750.00
Financial Services	$500.00	$3,000.00	
Furniture	$500.00	$10,000.00	$10,000.00
Gas/Heat	$1,440.00	$5,000.00	$250.00
Grand opening expense	$500.00	$10,000.00	$10,000.00
Graphic Design services	$500.00	$30,000.00	
Internet	$480.00	$2,000.00	$250.00
Lease-hold improvements	$500.00	$10,000.00	$2,000.00
Legal Services	$250.00	$10,000.00	$1,000.00
Liability/Building Insurance	$300.00	$2,000.00	$500.00
Licenses & Permits	$100.00	$2,500.00	$250.00
Lunches/Dinners/Client Meeting Cost's	$600.00	$5,000.00	
Merchant Services (Am. Ex. Visa, MC)	$300.00	$1,000.00	$500.00
Message Service	$500.00	$2,400.00	$250.00
Misc. (pre-opening expenses)	$100.00	$10,000.00	$1,000.00
Office Supplies	$1,200.00	$3,000.00	$250.00
Payroll taxes	$0.00	$15,000.00	$1,000.00
Phone (4 lines)	$900.00	$5,000.00	$500.00
Phone Maintenance	$500.00	$2,500.00	
Postage	$480.00	$5,760.00	$250.00
Printing Services	$360.00	$5,000.00	$250.00
Project Director	$30,000.00	$50,000.00	
Receptionist ($11.00 x 40 hrs)	$18,000.00	$25,000.00	
President	$20,000.00	$100,000.00	$20,000.00
Rent	$6,000.00	$24,000.00	$2,500.00
Restroom Accessories	$150.00	$2,000.00	$100.00
Sales Rep/Commission	$1,200.00	$30,000.00	
Security Deposits	$1,200.00	$5,000.00	$2,500.00
Signage	$0.00	$5,000.00	$2,000.00
Software & Misc. Computer Equipment	$100.00	$10,000.00	$5,000.00
Subscriptions	$20.00	$150.00	
Water	$360.00	$1,000.00	$50.00
Website/Email Services	$300.00	$5,000.00	$50.00
Workers Comp. Insurance	$120.00	$2,000.00	$500.00
Benefits for Staff (401 k, health Insurance, etc.)	$2,400.00	$10,000.00	$500.00
TOTAL COST:	$107,040.00	$590,310.00	$84,550.00

Estimated Profit Statement (Language Business) Example

INCOME (estimate)	Low Annual Estimate	High Annual Estimate
Translation Services (Document, Websites, Forms, etc.)	$100,000.00	$250,000.00
Interpreting Services (All languages, 24 hr service, weekends, etc.)	$100,000.00	$250,000.00
Consultation Fees (Strategic Planning, Cultural Review, Project Management)	$20,000.00	$50,000.00
Language Class (Spanish, French, English, etc.)	$20,000.00	$80,000.00
English as a Second Language (ESL) Class	$20,000.00	$75,000.00
Citizenship Assistance (Applying, Review, Preparation)	$30,000.00	$120,000.00
Misc.	$1,500.00	$50,000.00
TOTAL INCOME:	**$291,500.00**	**$875,000.00**

TOTAL PROFIT: *total costs on pg. 77

	Low Annual Estimate	High Annual Estimate
Expenses=(Subtract Total Costs from Total Income from above)	$193,040.00	$727,270.00
Total Profit	$98,460.00	$875,000.00
*PROFIT	**$98,460.00**	**$147,730.00**

1st Year Estimated Annual Profit
*Start Up Costs ($84,550.00) - Profit = 1st yr Annual Profit)

	Low Annual Estimate	High Annual Estimate
	$13,910.00	$63,180.00

This is an example. Costs will vary.

	Startup	Jan-10	Feb-10	Mar-10	Apr-10	May-10	Jun-10	Jul-10	Aug-10	Sep-10	Oct-10	Nov-10	Dec-10	Total Item EST
Cash on Hand (beginning of month)		0	0	0	0	0	0	0	0	0	0	0	0	0
CASH RECEIPTS														
Cash Sales														
Collections fm CR accounts														
Loan/ other cash inj.														
TOTAL CASH RECEIPTS	0	0	0	0	0	0	0	0	0	0	0	0	0	0
Total Cash Available (before cash out)	0	0	0	0	0	0	0	0	0	0	0	0	0	0
CASH PAID OUT														
Purchases (merchandise)														
Purchases (specify)														
Purchases (specify)														
Gross wages (exact withdrawal)														
Payroll expenses (taxes, etc.)														
Outside services														
Supplies (office & oper.)														
Repairs & maintenance														
Advertising														
Car, delivery & travel														
Accounting & legal														
Rent														
Telephone														
Utilities														
Insurance														
Taxes (real estate, etc.)														
Interest														
Other expenses (specify)														
Other (specify)														
Other (specify)														
Miscellaneous														
SUBTOTAL	0	0	0	0	0	0	0	0	0	0	0	0	0	0
Loan principal payment														
Capital purchase (specify)														
Other startup costs														
Reserve and/or Escrow														
Owners' Withdrawal														
TOTAL CASH PAID OUT	0	0	0	0	0	0	0	0	0	0	0	0	0	0
Cash Position (end of month)	0	0	0	0	0	0	0	0	0	0	0	0	0	0
ESSENTIAL OPERATING DATA (non cash flow information)														
Sales Volume (dollars)														
Accounts Receivable														
Bad Debt (end of month)														
Inventory on hand (eom)														
Accounts Payable (eom)														
Depreciation														

*"When it's a question of money,
everybody is of the same religion."*

— **Voltaire**
Writer & Philosopher

Chapter 13
WHAT DO YOU CHARGE TO DO...?

Rates, Fees and Other Billing Costs

"Translation Businesses, Independent Contractors and Freelancers live and die by the rates they charge, the agreements they develop and the policies they create to protect themselves from liability. Guard your rates with your life and do not under charge for your services."

- Sal Soto

DeSoto Translations, CEO &

President

I made the paragraph above extra large so that you would not miss it nor forget it. If you remember nothing else from this book than this one paragraph I have saved you thousands, if not millions of dollars in losses and legal costs.

Under Charging?

When I first started my company I had no clue what I was going to charge let alone if people would pay my rates once I established them. Where would I get these magic numbers from and how would I justify them? Why are language companies' rates higher than independent contractors/freelancers? What I soon learned was not only would my clients pay my rates there was always some cost's I forgot to include in my estimate- that is probably why I was out bidding my competitors, I was making very little to no profit on some projects and knew I had to do something or I would go out of business.

Additionally, there was always someone trying to find a way around paying for our services or for certain charges. Whether it was a client trying to get their project done in 1-day but refusing to pay a rush fee or a client asking to have translations saved on a disk and sent to them via FedEx overnight at my expense and inconvenience. From time to time there will be small cost you incur to keep your clients happy especially if they are spending a lot of money on your services. Undoubtedly there will be those clients that will continually and unfairly push expenses on you until you say no or you go out of business.

There have even been occasions we were told that the project was reviewed by someone "in-house" once it was delivered and that it didn't meet the "in-house" person's standards and that the client was simply not going to pay us for the project. We are talking thousands of dollars in losses; some companies have gone under because of one or two incidents like this happening in the same month or year. These were no small 1-page documents either; we're talking about 200 page technical manuals that had taken several people and several months to complete.

What did we do wrong? Could it be fixed? Were the expectations not met or were they not explained clearly? Did we have a signed agreement to ensure payment? Who was at fault and just who was this "in-house" person? What credentials did he or she have?

To make sure you do not find yourself in a similar situation this is one area of the business that I would encourage you to look at carefully and at the very least annually for revisions, updates and to asses costs that could and should be covered by your clients. In this chapter I have included a few samples of policies and agreements used to protect both you and the client from not having a clear understanding of each other's expectations, processes and policies.

Service Categories

There are 4 main service categories your projects will fall under in the language industry. On occasion some categories will overlap or if the project is large could involve 2 or more categories to accomplish the project. This is why it is important to track and manage all your projects.

4 Main Types of Language Industry Fees/Projects

1. Interpreter Projects & Fees

2. Translation Projects & Fees

3. Consultation Services & Fees

4. Miscellaneous Projects & fees (ex. Graphic design, layout, FedEx, Rush, etc.)

Basic Rates Example

TRANSALTION SERVICES

General Translations: (General Documents and Letters)

Rate: **$0.30 to $0.50 cents per word**

Minimum Charge: $50.00

Technical Translations: (Legal, Contracts, Agreements, Medical, Ad Agency)

Rate: **$0.40 to $0.60 cents per word**

Minimum Charge: $50.00

Editing & Proofreading: Rate: **$50 per hour**
Minimum Charge: 1 hour

Creative Review Consultation: **Flat Rate per Project**
Graphic Design:.Rate: **$50 to $100 per hour**
1/2 hour minimum

Layout: Rate: **$50 per hour**
1/2 hour minimum

INTERPRETING

General Interpreting Services:
All languages subject to availability
unless prior arrangements have been made   Rate: **$50 to 75 per hour**
Minimum 1 hour Charge

Mileage:(Outside of County-Current IRS Rate)   Rate: **$0.55 per mile**

Parking:(If applicable)   Rate: **Billed to Client**

ADDITIONAL FEES- Example

Courier Fee: (If applicable)   Rate: **Billed to Client**

Rush Fees: Requests need to be made a minimum of (2) business-days in advance to avoid 50%-150% rush charge.

Overnight Delivery for Copywriting and Translation Projects of up to 1,000 words (Spanish Guaranteed)……..Rate: 50%-150% additional to the corresponding standard rate.

Business Terms and Payment Conditions

A signed service agreement must be on file.

All revisions must be assigned within 30 days of receipt of the translation/copy.

Payment is due upon receipt of the project.

A late payment charge of 1.25% monthly (16.07% annually) is applied to all payments not received within 30 days of the invoice date.

For larger projects and for new clients ($1,000.00), we require 50% at the onset. The remainder is due at the completion of the contract.

Flat Billing is available for larger projects, public relations or advertising campaigns. The rate is directly related to the project's unique specifications. We will submit a written estimate.

Delivery times will be agreed on a per project basis (Overnight or rush service will be delivered as stated).

Payments can be made by credit card, check or cash

Here are some examples of services provided by "Full-Service"

Language Translation firms as well as freelancers:

1. Graphic design assistance
2. Proofreading
3. Layout of translation from source language to target language
4. Layout assistance
5. Website Localization
6. Cultural Content Review
7. Project management
8. On-site Interpreting
9. Phone interpreting
10. Conference call & Video Conference Interpreting

Additional Services You Can Charge For

Dictionary Creation

The creation of a "Dictionary of Terms." This dictionary will include terms, phrases and acronyms developed for the client/project. Most large projects will have several terms that do not translate well or not at all into the target language. It will be your job to research and assess possible word & phrase replacements.

Project Consultation Fee

Clients that are new to purchasing translation & interpreting services or developing interpreter networks for their company may need to be walked through the process. In a consultant role you will help them to understand the process and assist in the development of their initiative. Make sure the client is aware that anytime over 1 hour, which is customary in the industry, is time that will be billed for Project Consultation.

Project Management Fee

You could and should charge a Project Management Fee for projects that entail multiple languages or multiple projects. A 10%-25% fee added to the total cost of the project is standard.

Voice-Over/Voice Talent

Voice-Over Talent is different from your basic interpreter. This person will provide the voice talent for commercials, videos and radio spots. This type of bilingual talent is hard to find and should be billed accordingly. I have seen rates vary from $50 to $500 per hour depending on the client, project and language.

Quotes & Estimates

Free quotes and estimates are standard in the language industry. However, some projects are so large and multifaceted that creating a quote/estimate becomes a job all in itself. You should charge for the time it takes to create the quote or estimate in this case.

Converting projects from one program to another

From time to time a client will send you a project in a design file (Photoshop, IN design, PageMaker, Quark, etc.) and ask you to convert the project to Word or a program that is easier for you to work in. There will be times where you will need to buy the software they originally used so that you can insert or export the text and images to create a complete translation.

Tip

Call around and talk with local translation agencies, interpreters and designers to find out their rates for these types of services. If you outsource projects to these vendors it is customary to have them reduce their rate by 10%-15%. You can either charge your client the full rate of the vendor and keep the reduced percentage as a kind of "referral fee" or pass the savings along to your client to keep you overall rate for the project low.

General Pricing Guidelines for Translations

There is no correct or standard (yet) way to bill for your services at the moment. However, here are a few rules of thumb I have noticed:

1. **More words** = lower rate per word
   Less words = higher rate per word

2. **Less technical** = lower rate per word
   More technical = higher rate per word

3. **Longer turn around time** = lower cost per word
   Shorter turn around time = higher cost per word

*Discount System should be based on volume and nothing else.

I have seen some translators give their potential clients the opportunity to make an informed decision by presenting a two-fold estimate of final charges. They indicate a minimum charge and also a maximum one that is agreed not to exceed.

Minimum "per page" Translation Pricing Example

I have noted that one page (approximately 500 words) of an informal document, takes a translator approximately one hour to translate. If you were to charge an average cost of $50 per hour, a 1-page informal document of about 500 words would cost $50. However, in order to give you a precise price quote to which you will agree to, you should always review the actual document, or a representative sample as well as the turnaround time and language. The range in cost reflects differences in content and format between documents. Certain projects demand more time and effort than others and therefore should cost more.

Notary/Certified Translations

Notarization requires additional time and procedures that include printing a hard copy, having a Notary Public notarize the document, then mailing the document to the client or having them come to your office to pick it up. You could charge an additional $30.00-$50.00 for the first notarized document in addition to the translation fee and $10.00 each for any other notarized documents in the same project. *You are NOT Charging for the Notary Public stamp, you are charging for your time. In some states it is illegal to charge for Notary Public services.

A Certified Translation is a fully reviewed, professional, quality translation to which the translator declares that he or she is fluent in both the source and target language(s), and certifies that the translation is complete and accurate to the best of the translator's knowledge and ability. You will need to have a corporate stamp similar to a Notary Public stamp for this type of "certified" translation which can cost $100-$500 to have made.

Most local signage and stamp shops will have exact costs and designs. *DeSoto Representatives can login to their DeSoto Translations website account to purchase a DeSoto Corporate Stamp or to become a Notary Public at: www.DESOTOTRANSLATIONS.com

Some institutions, especially universities and government agencies require sworn or notarized translations.

Examples of documents that need to be notarized or certified are:

1. Immigration and Naturalization Service
2. Birth/Death & Marriage Certificates
3. Divorce Documents
4. Department of Internal Affairs
5. Department of Motor Vehicles
6. Embassies & Consulate Office
7. Justice Department and most Courts
8. Diplomas & Transcripts
9. Etc .

Word Expansion & Reduction

Spanish uses up to 20% more words than English. English can be characterized as a "telegraphic" language, meaning one that requires relatively fewer words to express the same idea in Spanish or other languages.

This is one of the many reason why charging by the page can be misleading since the amount of text varies from one document to another and from one language to another. The width of the margins, the size of the script/font, the presence of graphics, the "leading" between lines, and these variables impact the amount of work. I have included a sample of a language expansion chart that is standard in the language industry.

See Word Expansion Chart on the Following Page

Language Expansion Chart- Sample

Visit www.DESOTOTRANSLATIONS.com for an Up-to-Date list

Arabic	English	Approximately equal
Bosnian	English	Word count x 1.15
Bulgarian	English	Word count x 1.15
Cambodian	English	Character count x 0.17
Chinese	English	Character count x 0.72
Croation	English	Word count x 1.15
Czech	English	Word count x 1.15
Danish	English	Word count x 1.20
Dutch	English	Word count x 1.15
English	Arabic	Use Englishword count
English	Bosnian	Word count x 0.95
English	Bulgarian	Word count x 1.1
English	Cambodian (Khmer)	Use Englishword count
English	Chinese	Use Englishword count
English	Croation	Word count x 0.95
English	Czech	Word count x 0.95
English	Danish	Word count x 0.95
English	Dutch	Word count x 1.05
English	Estonian	Word count x 0.85
English	Farsi	Use Englishword count
English	Finnish	Word count x 0.80
English	Flemish	Word count x 1.05
English	French	Word count x 1.25
English	Georgian	Word count x 0.80
English	German	Word count x 0.95
English	Greek	Word count x 1.10
English	Hebrew	Use Englishword count
English	Hmong	Word count x 1.4
English	Hungarian	Word count x 0.95
English		Use Englishword count
English	Indonesian	Word count x 1.20
English	Italian	Word count x 1.25
English	Japanese	Use Englishword count
English	Kazakh	Word count x 0.85
English	Khmer	Use Englishword count
English	Korean	Use Englishword count
English	Lao	Use Englishword count
English	Latvian	Word count x 0.95
English	Malay	Word count x 1.20
English	Norwegian	Word count x 0.90
English	Polish	Word count x 1.10
English	Portuguese	Word count x 1.20
English	Russian	Word count x 1.10
English	Serbian	Word count x 0.95
English	Slovak	Word count x 0.95
English	Slovene	Word count x 0.95
English	Somali	Word count x 1.25
English	Spanish	Word count x 1.25
English	Swedish	Word count x 0.95
English	Tagalog	Word count x 1.25
English	Thai	Use Englishword count
English	Turkish	Word count x 0.90

Discounted Rates for Not For Profits & High Volume Clients

Some individuals and agencies in the language industry charge a lower rate for non-profit organizations (such as social service agencies, NGOs, community volunteer associations, etc.) that are not involved in commerce and for clients that account for a large amount of their annual business. Average discounted rate is between 10%-20% off the standard rates. *Note: There may be materials and services that you outsource or purchase at cost that cannot be discounted.*

Scheduling & Deadlines

An average translator can translate 2000 words (or more) in one day depending on the nature of the document. Large projects are usually assigned to teams of 2-3 people to get the project done faster. Make sure you discuss scheduling and deadlines with your client as well as the additional "Rush" fee they may incur. Evidently, conventional mail will add several days before and after the translation. If you send digitized documents, it will speed up time.

Formatting & Layout Assistance

Most people use Word or Excel to create text documents. This program will accept documents written with many different processors, including WordPerfect, MAC, and a number of others, including ASCII. Due to the nature of the two languages (and certain explanatory additions and terms in both languages), Spanish and several other languages tends to take up to 10%-20% more words/space than the equivalent in English.

This fact could affect your layout. Also, several clients will want you to take their graphic design files and extract the English text, then insert the translated text. Be up front if this is something you can't do, design programs can be tricky if you are not familiar with them. Rates for this service range from $50-$200 per hour depending on the graphic designer/ graphic design company.

Proofreading

It is important to have a stringent proofreading and quality control process in place. Do not forget to review the project after sending it to your client or before it is printed to ensure all the accent marks, images and special characters you included in the final project are in the correct places. On occasion characters, fonts and images go missing during the conversion process from one version of the same program to another. (Special fonts and accent marks could be lost when converting from Word 93-2000 to Word for Vista). Always offer, demanding might come off as rude, to review and sign-off on the final proof from the printers. Several mistakes and errors could be overted if this process were to take place after each translation project was completed.

Languages are inherently ambiguous. Entire thoughts can be interpreted in more than one way. Therefore I like to stay in close touch with my clients to insure that what they mean in one language will be completely and accurately expressed in the other

There is an extensive resource list at the back of this book. Also, visit the website www.desototranslations.com for more up-to-date information as well as Up-to-Date Rates and services.

"Money is not the only answer,
but it makes a difference"

— **Barack Obama**
President of the United States

Chapter 14
DEVELOPING RATES FOR INTERPRETERS & FREELANCERS
Creating & Understanding Your Rates

Interpreters and translators spend an inordinate and disproportionate amount of time determining pricing and fretting over it. But there is no right or wrong answer when it comes to pricing. It's all completely subjective and dependent on a wide variety of factors. Getting pricing right could be defined as charging enough to ensure good profitability, but not so much as to lose a client to competition. In this chapter, we'll cover the nuts and bolts of estimating a project and figuring out how much to charge.

Understanding What You Are Selling

One major obstacle for many linguists and language business owners is the belief that what you charge is related to your value as a person. Wrong! First of all, it's not about you. A prospect or client will often ask, "How much do you charge for the translation of a web site?" or "How much do you charge to translate a brochure?" or "How much do you charge for… fill-in-the-blank?" as if they are buying a box of cupcakes. Look at the way that question is constructed: "How much do you charge for…"

If you were selling artwork, and somebody said, "How much do you charge for a painting?" you wouldn't say "I charge $1000 for a painting." You would say, "It depends on the painting. Could you be more specific? If you'd like I could meet with you to understand your request, budget and timeframe."

It's the same with language services. It has nothing to do with what "you charge." It's not about you, and it never will be. Shift your mindset to think instead about what the product and the process costs. When someone says, "How much do you charge to translate a web site?" take the "you" out of it and respond with, "A web site translation can cost $X."

You're Not Selling Your Time

Time flies when you're doing your work, especially on the projects you really enjoy. In fact, you may not notice how much time you're spending. Some translators don't realize they've spent much more time than they had initially allowed for. They don't dare divide the number of hours by their hourly rate, only to discover they're making little more than minimum wage. That's a rude awakening. And it's all the more reason to track your time.

It's a cliché, but it's true: Time is money. The more time one project takes, the less time you have for another, and the less money you make.

What you are selling is your years of experience, the effort you've expended developing your skills and talents, and your resulting expertise. What you are selling is peace of mind. Not many clients understand language, so they don't know what they're buying, and they know they don't know. So it's your job to make them comfortable and safe in the knowledge that you do understand and will take care of everything. If you do that, the good clients will choose you, even if you're the highest bidder.

What you are selling is your brain, your attention, your quality and accuracy process that is applied to a client's specific problem and that has a value. It's not an objective value; in fact, it's highly subjective, which makes it challenging to quantify.

That "value" is based on several factors, including geographic location, timing, what the market will bear, the urgency of your prospect's need, aggravation factor (or lack thereof), what it's worth to you to do it, and your level of desperation (hopefully low to nonexistent), just to name a few. It is important to review what the rates are in your area especially to understand what your clients have been paying.

You may find that they were getting a hell of a deal because the person before you set the market price so low because they were working from home, took several weeks to complete small projects, depended on the income of a spouse to pay for bills and had little training. In essence, providing language services was a hobby for this person, not a business. You will have to spend some time educating your clients on the difference between what they did and what you do.

The Value of Your Work

There is no intrinsic value to your work. Its value is based on perceptions. The perceived value of any project comes as a result of positioning your services properly through your marketing and sales process. You have to understand your client well to know what she will find valuable. Maybe he or she cares most how well the project is executed. Or that you meet all the deadlines. Or that you deliver quality, ease, and time or saved the person some stress? Once you know what's important to each of your clients, you can position yourself to provide exactly that. And they will pay for it.

Value comes with service, not translation. Translations have become a commodity. Your clients can get it almost anywhere. Sometime they can do it themselves. (How many times have you heard a client say they've got a bilingual employee that they are thinking of using to save money?) Your competitors are up and down the pricing spectrum. There will always be someone whose price is lower, so you must understand what value you add, and use that to position your services.

Customer service will help you stand apart. You add value by anticipating needs, by under-promising and over-delivering. That's why they appreciate it when you take the lead. They want you to be in charge so they can focus on other things. That's how you sell peace of mind through language services.

The Importance of an Hourly Rate

In order to run a healthy and profitable business, you must know how long it takes you to do various tasks and projects; in essence, you must know your expenses, and time is a major expense. If you're just starting out in business, you'll probably be guessing at first, and you'll make lots of mistakes-that's the good news.

You should be tracking your time and that of any freelancer or employee who works for you. If you've been at this for a while, your timesheets or time tracking forms & software will give you detailed reports of what you spend (time, money and materials) on each project.

Your hourly rate is not your only cost, though. It's one of the building blocks of your price, so you need to know what it is. Your time is what you track, and it should be the basis of your pricing, though only for internal purposes. In other words, use your hourly rate to determine what to charge for a project, but never reveal that hourly rate in a proposal or in conversations with your client. Not only is it none of their business, it also wouldn't mean anything to them. An hourly rate is only relevant in relation to how long a project takes, and they have no idea how long design takes. You open the door to their assumptions by talking about your hourly rate in detail.

So when a client asks you how long a project will take, never say, "This will take X hours." The only thing they need to know about time is when they can expect to receive the deliverable.

What I would recommend you say instead is, "Let me check what we have on the schedule, and I'll get back to you with a time frame. In the meantime, let me know your deadline and I will do my best to accommodate it."

Salary and Overhead

Once you have an accurate hourly rate, it should be used as the basis for your project fees-again, though, only for internal purposes.

At the end of the day, you have to know how much you must charge, which is different from how much you should charge. What you should charge is up to you and takes into consideration how much others charge for the services-what's competitive and what's not. In addition to your translation, proofreading and other fees, there are other elements of a project that must be factored into the price. Your salary and overheard are two crucial components.

Many self-employed people do not include their salaries in the overhead; they see their salaries as the profit they take out of the business. But salaries are a business expense. Profit comes after all expenses are paid, including all salaries. **The rule is to pay yourself first.**

To determine a number for your salary, ask yourself how much you want to make in a year, realistically. Set attainable goals, and keep raising the bar. That's how you get to six figures or a million or whatever your dream number is. Also included in your overhead are all the expenses required to keep the doors open. It's the cost of doing business, including your computer, the monthly phone bill, insurance, maintenance, supplies and computer software. Some are fixed expenses that don't fluctuate from month to month; others depend entirely on usage, which you can control.

Calculating Your Business Overhead

COSTS (You can calculate this either by month or by year)

Automobile

Fuel

Insurance and Registration

Car payment/Lease

Parking

Repairs and Maintenance

Subtotal:_____

Insurance

Health and dental

Tax Liability

Worker's comp

Subtotal:_____

OFFICE EXPENSES

Internet Access

Licenses

Business Phone and Fax

Mobile Phone

Web Hosting and E-mail Hosting

Rent

Utilities

Supplies

Computers

Software

Subtotal:_____

TRAVEL EXPENSES

Hotels

Airfare

Rental Cars

Subtotal:_____

MARKETING

E-mail Marketing Service

Postage

Printing

Client Dining

Client Gifts

Copywriting

Subtotal:_____

BUSINESS SERVICE/PERSONNEL FEES

Accounting

Lawyer/legal Fees

Bookkeeping

Subtotal:_____

EMPLOYEES

Salaries

Medical Benefits

Taxes

Other Employee Costs

Subtotal:_____

OTHER EXPENSES

Misc. 1

Misc. 2

Subtotal:_____

TOTAL OVERHEAD:_____

What Will Your Profit Be?

Once you know your overhead, the next question is: How much profit do you want to earn? Ten percent? Twenty percent? Your profit is not tied to how much time the project takes; it is built into your hourly rate. If, however, once you have estimated for a potential project, the number you come up with feels too low, or if the client's budget allows for more, you are free to add additional profit. Again, you're in business, among other things, to make money.

Most entrepreneurs will tell you, profit is a business necessity, not a luxury. Among other things, profit allows a firm to fund a reserve against times of slow business, to provide for future capital requirements, and to give principals compensation beyond their salaries as a return for investment risk.

How to Figure Your Hourly Rate

Most interpreters and translators wonder if they're charging enough. You probably do, too. And you probably aren't. Where does your hourly rate come from? Out of thin air? From an industry guide? Is it a number that's close to or the same as what your competition charges? Is it a number you chose because it's comfortable to you and no one complains about it?

If you're getting every job you bid on, you're probably not charging enough. Or did you sit down and figure out how much you need to charge in order to earn the living you need and achieve your goals? For most people, the answer to that last question is no. But if you don't figure out what your hourly rate must be in order to cover your expenses, how will you know if you are charging enough?

6 Steps To Figure Out Your Hourly Rate

*There is a sample form at the end of this chapter

Step 1: Determine your salary. That's right, you get to decide. What is the salary you need your business to pay you, before taxes? Let's work with $40,000. This is the "100 percent" figure that corresponds to the example at the end of this chapter. Add 30 percent on top of that to cover your income tax. Thirty percent of $40,000 is $12,000. Therefore, you need to pull $52,000 per year from your business in order to get your desired salary.

Step 2: Figure your labor hourly rate. That is how much money you make for every hour that you work, or, more accurately, for every hour that you bill a client. To do that, determine how many hours you'll be working for clients. To do that, determine how many hours you'll be working for clients in a year.

1,142 hours is an industry standard used for figuring hourly rates, and it's based on a 40-hour work week. If you're working part-time, figure it based on the number of hours you actually work per week.

Based on a standard 40-hour work week, there are 2,080 working hours in a year (52 weeks x 40 hours per week). In reality, however, people get sick and take days off. The standard number used for days off is 176 hours (that's 22 eight-hour days). So, 2,080 working hours – 176 days off = 1,904 working hours in the year.

That doesn't mean you're billing all 1, 904 hours. If your business is healthy and thriving, you'll spend approximately 40 percent of your time on administrative duties, managing, invoicing, filing, marketing, travel, and so forth. That means 60 percent of your time is billable. Sixty percent of 1,904 is 1,142.

To calculate your hourly rate, take the total salary you need ($52,000) and divide it by 1,142 hours. That brings your labor hourly rate to $45.53. If you work and bill 1,142 hours at this rate you'll make the after-tax income of $40,000 you want.

Step 3: Determine your business overhead by adding up all your expenses. (See Business Overhead Worksheet at beginning of this chapter) It's very important that you understand how much it costs to run your business. A lot of people, especially solo entrepreneurs, underestimate this. If you work from home, your home and business expenses probably get mixed together. Plus, working from home, you don't "feel" the expenses as much as you would if you worked in an office and had to write separate checks for things such as rent, phone and Internet.

That's why it's important to separate the two. You should have a business checking account and understand what percentage of your home expenses actually are business expenses. If you had to go out tomorrow and rent an office and not use the convenience of home, how much would that cost? If you are spending $35,000 a year on a business that's paying you only $40,000, your business expenses are really high and you should look for places to cut expenses.

Step 4: Make sure your hourly rate covers your overhead. Your overhead hourly rate is what you must charge just to cover your overhead. You determine this by first figuring what percentage of your total salary is the business overhead. So take the overhead $35,000 and divide it by the total salary. $52,000, which in this example is 67.3 percent. That's your overhead hourly rate.

Multiply that percentage (67.3) percent by your labor hourly rate ($45.53) to find out how much to add to cover not only your salary, but also your expenses. In this example, $30.64 an hour will cover overhead.

Step 5: Add your labor hourly rate to your overhead hourly rate to find the total hourly rate required to cover both your salary and your overhead.

So: $45.53 + $30.64= $76.17.

Step 6: Add your profit. You're working to make a profit, right? It's up to you how much profit your want to make. Ten to twenty percent is standard. In this example, we'll add a 10 percent profit. So, add 10 percent to the combined labor and overhead rate to get $83.79. Round it up to $85 an hour.

There you have it. You have just calculated your hourly rate.

So your business is thriving, and if you're billing 1,142 hours at $85 per hour, after business expenses and taxes, you will take home the $40,000 that you want, plus a 10 percent profit. Now, $85 is the base hourly rate to work with. It's not necessarily what you should be charging; it's the minimum you must charge to run this business profitably. Once you calculate this rate for yourself, you'll know the base of how much you'll have to figure into a project. You must charge *at least* this much. You can charge more-as much more as you like.

If you're figuring out an hourly rate for a two-person studio, you simply double the 1,142 hours becomes 2,284 hours. Since the salary has to be doubled, the available hours have to be doubled. But there should be only one business overhead number because it's the overhead for the whole business.

YOUR HOURLY RATE (example)

STEP 1

A. Estimated salary
ex: $40,000
yours:_____

B. Estimated taxes (add 30%)
ex: $12,000
yours:_____

C. Total salary for the year
ex: $52,000
yours:_____

D. Yearly business hours
ex: 2,080, or 1,904 after vacation and sick days
yours:_____

E. 60% billable efficiency
ex: 1.142 billable hours per year
yours:_____

STEP 2

F. Labor hourly rate: total salary /billable hours (line C/ line E)
ex: $45.53
yours:_____

STEP 3

G. Business overhead expenses
ex: $35,000
yours:_____

H. Business overhead + salary (line C + line G)
ex: $87,000
yours:_____

STEP 4

I. Overhead as % of salary (line G/line C)
ex: 67.3%
yours:_____

STEP 5

J. Overhead hourly rate: labor hourly rate x overhead % (line F x line J)
ex: $30.64
yours:_____

K. Rate to recover income + overhead: (line F + line K)
ex: $76.17
yours:_____

That is what you must charge; now add your profit.

STEP 6

L. Profit percentage: hourly rate x 10%
ex: $7.62
yours:_____

M. Add that to your hourly rate
ex: $83.79
yours:_____

This is what you should charge per hour. Then round it up:

ex: $85.00
yours:_____

Other Factors to Consider

Project Management

Every job will involve some level of project management, and it will differ according to the complexity of the project. Translating a website in one language will generally require the involvement of fewer people than translating 5 websites, 5 brochure's and 5 newsletters in 5 languages at the same time for the same client. That's why you must charge extra for project management. Don't give away your time; build it into the final number.   Add a percentage of hours that you think it will take to manage the project. That percentage comes from your experience and your tracking, but if you don't have much of either one, start with 25 percent to be safe, then keep track and see if that's accurate.

Revisions

The ideal job may be one where you complete your translations and the client has no updates or revisions. Alas, this doesn't happen often, which is why you must allow for revisions in your estimate. But how many rounds of revisions should you allow for? This is another mystery, especially when working with new clients. I usually allow for revisions (less than 10% of the total word count) and updates. However, they must be made within 30 days of receipt of the final project.

Anything above the agreed amount and time frame for revisions is charged at your "revision hourly rate." This is yet another hourly rate. It should be no less than your standard hourly rate and probably a bit higher. It could also be very high-as high as $300 an hour-because it should convey this message: "We don't want to do revisions." Do your best to avoid several unexpected rounds of revisions. They are problematic for everyone involved. If you tell your client early on what the revision hourly rate is, they are likely to avoid most revisions and provide you with the final copy that is complete and accurate.

Markup

Markup is an amount added by a seller (you) to the cost of a commodity to cover expenses and profit in fixing the selling price. It's like a broker fee that you take for facilitating a process. It is standard business practice to add a markup on anything that you have to oversee and coordinate that is not already covered by your hourly rate, including layout, design, copy insertion, printing, hard-copy "proofs," mailing, and copywriting.

Some translators and interpreters feel insecure about charging a markup. You may feel it's deceptive, that you don't deserve it. Forget all that. You're not stealing or gouging your clients. At the grocery store, you can be sure you're not paying what the grocer paid. Standard markup at retail is often 100 percent or more. Every time something goes through another pair of hands, a layer of fees is added. This is business, and your clients understand and probably even expect it.

You needn't disclose your markup in any way that calls extra attention to it. It's built in to your pricing and there will likely not be questions. And if, on occasion, a client resists paying a markup, you can offer to let them take care of that aspect of the project on their own, whether it's printing, layout or something else. Standard markup in the language industry is 20-50 percent, depending on several factors, including who the client is, the size of the company, where you are located and what they would pay for the services or products if they procured them directly.

Rush Charges

Clients can have a rush job for a variety of reasons, such as shift in priorities or an opportunity that arises out of the blue. But often, it's due to a lack of planning. The project was sitting on their desks for six months before it rose to the top of pile. If you don't charge rush fees, you will pay the price for their lack of planning. Standard rush charges start at 50 percent, but it can sometimes go as high as 100 percent. The rule is that the less time you have to work on the project (deadline), the higher the percentage you charge for the rush.

Clients know rush means more money, whether they acknowledge it or not. This can be a fuzzy area because there is no standard for what constitutes a rush. That's why you need to establish what your normal pace is and what a rush is. You also need to let your clients know from the moment they say, "I needed this like yesterday", this situation qualifies as a rush. In fact, make a description of this process accessible to clients; you can even publish it on your web site or on your estimates.

Rushing generally adds chaos to a project, so everything you can do to bring order will eliminate potential for miscommunication, or worse. When a client is in a hurry, the estimating process often gets shortened, sometimes even skipped over altogether in the interest of time. But this is not in anyone's best interest, including your client's. Take the time to go through your regular process; simply speed it up due to the circumstances. Always provide a written estimate, even it's an abbreviated one, and insist that your client sign off on it before beginning the work. Sometimes an e-mail agreement is enough, especially for a current client. Whatever the medium, simply say, "I am sending you the agreement today, and I will need your approval and a deposit before we start the work." Don't forgo the deposit. They may have reasons why they can't get the deposit to you quickly. Consider this a red flag and don't back down. Simply ask, "What can we do to secure this project?" Offering the option to pay by credit card could speed things along.

Be happy to get a rush job because rush jobs are very lucrative, especially if you are well organized. In fact, you can position your services with a focus on quick turnaround, and people will pay extra for it. That, in itself, could set you apart from the crowd.

If you don't want to do rush jobs, then you must train your clients to think and plan ahead. When you have clients whose projects are seasonal or regular, don't wait for them to initiate the process. Be proactive, create a schedule and keep them on track. Let them know with plenty of advance warning that they'll pay rush charges if they don't get started soon. Stay on top of it, and take the lead. You may also want to create a policy regarding accuracy and quality since you may have little time to complete your standard proofreading process. Clients will have to decide whether they want to sacrifice quality for the sake of getting the project done faster. It is ultimately up to the client which is most important.

Volume Discount

In some industries, it is customary to offer a discount to clients who do a lot of business- In essence, an incentive whereby the more they buy, the less they pay. This makes sense for printed or manufactured goods because it costs less to make more. But that isn't usually the case with language services. More work requires more time.

Sometimes, however, there is a savings and you are free to pass it along to your client. For example, if they have three related projects, such as a rebranding, a web site and a printed brochure based on the new branding, you can offer it a la carte or as a package deal. "If you sign off on all three right now, we'll take X percent off the total. "Sometimes this helps in the selling process. Plus, it helps your cash flow, too. If you do decide to offer this, make the offer when you first present the proposal, not in response to a pricing objection further along in the process.

"Our success has really been based on partnerships from the very beginning."

— Bill Gates
Founder of Microsoft

Chapter 15
PROJECT MANAGEMENT

Who's In Charge Here?

Your project types and sizes will vary in complexity so it is important to have a good understanding of how to manage projects so that you can successfully complete the assignments and contracts you receive.

The Five Project Management Processes

The following sections list the process completed during the lifecycle of any project and the rules you should keep in mind to get things done on time and within budget.

The Initiating Processes

➢ Identifying stakeholders including initial members of the project implementation team

➢ Recognizing that a project is worth doing

➢ Deciding that the risks associated with the project are appropriate to probable success

➢ Determining what the project should accomplish

➢ Defining the overall project goals

➢ Defining general expectations of customers, management, or other stakeholders, as appropriate

➢ Defining the general project scope

➢ Developing the statement of work (SOW) that documents the approved deliverables and the operational guidelines for the project.

The Planning Processes

> ➢ Refining the project scope, which includes identifying the balance required among results, time, resources, and project quality

> ➢ Listing task and activities that will lead to achieving the project goals

> ➢ Sequencing activities in the most efficient manner possible

> ➢ Developing a workable schedule and budget for assigning resources to the activities required to complete the project

> ➢ Getting the plan approved by the appropriate stakeholders

The Executive Processes

> ➢ Leading the team

> ➢ Meeting with team members

> ➢ Communicating with stakeholders

> ➢ Fire-fighting (also known as conflict resolution) to resolve problems that always arise during a project

> ➢ Securing necessary resources (money, people, equipment) to carry out the project plan

The Controlling Processes

> ➢ Monitoring project progress and deviation from the plan

> ➢ Taking corrective action to handle the day-to-day obstacles and problems that all projects seem to run into

> ➢ Receiving and evaluating project changes requested from stakeholders and team members

> ➢ Rescheduling the project if necessary to meet resource or outcome constraints

> ➢ Adapting resources levels as necessary to achieve on-time delivery of project outcomes

> ➢ Changing the project scope to meet project goals (but only when this is an appropriate and acceptable response)

> ➢ Returning to the planning stage to make adjustments to the project plan when necessary to get changes approved by the stakeholders

> ➢ Documenting and gaining approval for all changes to plans and project specifications so no one is surprised at the final outcome

The Closing Processes

➢ Shutting down the operations and disbanding the team

➢ Learning from the project experience

➢ Reviewing the project process and outcomes with team members and stakeholders

➢ Writing a final project report

The 12 Golden Rules of Project Management Success

1. Thou Shalt Gain Consensus on Project Outcomes.
2. Thou Shalt Build the Best Team You Can.
3. Thou Shalt Develop a Comprehensive, Viable Plan and Keep It Up to Date.
4. Thou Shalt Determine How Much Stuff You Really Need to Get Things Done.
5. Thou Shalt Have a Realistic Schedule.
6. Thou Shalt Not Try to Do More than Can Be Done.
7. Thou Shalt Remember that People Count.
8. Thou Shalt Gain the Formal and Ongoing Support of Management and Stakeholders.
9. Thou Shalt be Willing to Change.
10. Thou Shalt Keep People Informed of What you're Up To.
11. Thou Shalt Be Willing to Try New Things.
12. Thou Shalt Become a Leader as Well as a Manager.

The Project Success Factors

Within the framework of project management, there are really only three critical success factors:

1. **On-Time delivery**. Delivering the project according to an agreed-upon schedule.

2. **Within-Budget Delivery**. The project meets forecasted cost estimates.

3. **High-Quality Delivery**. The product or end result products must be of an agreed-upon high quality. In project management this means that the outcomes meet both the functional and performance features defined for the project.

Note: This list was adapted from The Idiots Guide to Project Management.

"An incompetent lawyer can delay a trial for months or years. A competent lawyer can delay one even longer."

— **Evelle Younger**
Attorney General California
1971-1979

Chapter 16
CONTRACTS & CONTRACTORS
The Devil is in the Details

You can't do everything yourself. If you try to, your business will remain very small, and the tasks you don't get done will either go undone or be done below par. That's why one reality of being self employed is that you need to identify your strengths, and then get help with your weaknesses. Even if you want your business to be small, recognize that it is limiting, too.

One way to get help is to hire freelancers a.k.a., contractors or sub-contractors. In fact, it's smart to have a pool of resources available and on call when you need them, so you don't have to go searching in your moment of need and make a quick decision without enough information or past experience related to their work ethic, quality and skill.

Most freelancers work on an hourly rate. They can come to your office, or they can work in their own spaces. You can decide which makes the most sense for your needs. But when it comes to paying freelancers, pay project fees rather than hourly rates, whenever possible. This is for the same reasons you should be charging project fees rather than an hourly rate: You hire them for their talent and their output, not how much time they spend. When you have a budget from a client, you can't simply give a subcontractor a blank slate.

Contractors are the bread and butter of any company that uses them. You need them more than you know and even more than they know. Unless you plan on having an enormous office, you can't possibly have all language services in house; therefore you must sub-contract "out" jobs and services to other people that are more skilled in each area and language.

Selecting contractors to translate or interpret projects is even more important because the accuracy and thoroughness of their work will directly affect your company's profits and reputation. Remember that your contractors are representing you as the owner of the company, so their work, rather good or bad, comes back on you in the end.

When you are outsourcing translation and interpreting projects, keep a few things in mind when choosing contractors to work with:

1. Good translators can both speak and write well. The most important thing is that a translator can accurately translate the language and not lose the context of the project. It is important that they understand the text before even attempting the translation. They communicate with you in the way you would communicate with your colleagues and customers. It's obvious from their speech and behavior that they are well trained and qualified.

2. Knowledgeable translators know where to find the information they will need to provide an accurate translation, and have invested in other essential resources that enable them to work quickly and efficiently such as dictionaries and computer tools.

3. Good translators take their work and their customers seriously, and present themselves in a businesslike manner. They are experienced and can provide professional credentials and references.

4. Good translators can give you an estimate of how long a job will take to translate, and how much it will cost, provided you let the translator know exactly what the job entails. They are also aware of their own capabilities and limitations. A smart translator should not take a job if they cannot do it competently and should instead refer you to someone who can complete the project as assigned.

5. Good translators are versatile and eager to learn. They are willing to invest time and energy in learning more about a new field; which can include getting certified and going to new training sessions.

6. Good translators ask questions. There is such a thing as a stupid question, but a good translator knows the right ones to ask. You'll be a busy person running around managing your company and you really can't be bothered with every detail. A smart translator will ask only the important questions and figure the rest out on their own.

When I first started I didn't have a clear agreement with my contractors and that caused so many unnecessary headaches and problems. First and foremost, you need a specific understanding between you and your contractors so the first step is acknowledging and articulating this understanding.

The second thing is to make sure to run your ideas and parameters by a lawyer that you feel are fair. Salaries, working conditions, and availability are common misconceptions between contractors and owners. Remember that since the person is on contract and not a full time employee, they can pick and take translation projects as they choose and you cannot force anything on them.

Explaining the agreement is essential. Make sure your contractors understand the agreement and everything that is expected of them so that there is no confusion and no surprises. Be fair, but at the same time protect your interests. Include a clause that contractors cannot steal your accounts (Ex. Non-Compete, Non-Soliciation, Anti-Poaching Agreement, etc.) with other companies that you have existing relationships with.

Contract Examples are on the following pages.

*If you are a DeSoto Translations Representative/Licensee visit the DeSoto website for contract and agreement downloads.

www.DESOTOTRANSLATIONS.com

Translation Contract & Agreement Samples

Company XYZ Translations Terms and Conditions

A translation order is a binding agreement between the Client ("the Client") and XYZ Translations ("XYZ"), covered by the following terms and conditions ("Terms and Conditions"):

1. INTENDED USE
1) When the Client does not indicate the intended use of the translation, XYZ shall execute the translation as if it were for information only. However, if in XYZ's judgment the apparent intended purpose is otherwise, XYZ shall communicate with the Client if possible in order to clarify the intended purpose before beginning translation.

2) If the Client wants to use a translation for a purpose other than that for which it was originally supplied, the Client shall obtain confirmation from XYZ that it is suitable for the new purpose. XYZ reserves the right to revise the previously supplied translation if necessary, at the Client's cost.

2. PROFESSIONAL STANDARD
1) XYZ will provide a clear and accurate translation, but cannot guarantee conformance to the subjective preference of the Client.

2) XYZ uses all available measures to ensure translation accuracy, but shall not be held liable for damages due to error or negligence in translation, transcription or formatting. Ultimate responsibility rests with the Client.

3. ESTIMATES & QUOTES
Cost is determined based on XYZ's current price list and the number of words in the source text. Written quotations are valid for 30 days. Verbal estimates are not binding and are subject to written confirmation on receipt of the text for translation.

4. PAYMENT
All orders pending credit approval. In the event of an unfavorable credit report, a 100% advanced payment is required before translation begins. Payment terms are net 21 days in US dollars, by US check or money order. Wire transfers are subject to a $25 fee. Late payments will be assessed a penalty of 1.5% per month. Costs of collection efforts including but not limited to collection agency fees and/or attorney fees incurred during the collection process will be the responsibility of the Client. All disputes shall be brought within the territorial jurisdiction of (State you live in). On receipt of payment, the copyright will be transferred to the Client.

All first orders under $500 require prepayment by credit card. An account is opened for a client only if a subsequent single order exceeds $500. Any exceptions are at XYZ's discretion.

5. ORDERS
By placing an order or submitting a purchase order to XYZ, the Client indicates acceptance of the Terms and Conditions at the time of the order. XYZ reserves the right to change the Terms and Conditions without notice. It is the Client's responsibility to check the Terms and Conditions prior to placing an order or submitting a purchase order to XYZ.

6. TRANSLATION DELIVERY
XYZ's date given for delivery is an estimate only. XYZ will make every endeavor to meet the date, but shall not be liable for any damage or loss arising directly or indirectly from its failure to meet such an estimated date. The Client may, at any time after such date, give XYZ reasonable notice regarding an expected delivery period of not less than seven days. If delivery does not take place within that period, the Contract will be considered cancelled and no charge will be made. If the translation is delivered after this period of notice passes and the Client does not rescind the cancellation of the Contract, XYZ requires the immediate return of the translation and a signed disclaimer of the Client's right to use the same. XYZ reserves the right to subcontract all or part of the work to a contractor(s) of its choice.

Delivery occurs upon transmission by email, fax, FTP or standard mail, and the risk passes to the Client. XYZ shall retain a copy of the translation and in the event of any loss or damage will forward an additional copy free of charge.

7. NATUARL DISASTER

In the event of Major Disaster (Natural Disaster, Acts of War or any other situation that materially affects XYZ's ability to deal with the Client's order) XYZ shall notify the Client immediately of the circumstances. Major Disasters shall entitle both XYZ and the Client to cancel the order, but the Client will pay XYZ for work already completed. XYZ will make every reasonable effort to place the Client's order elsewhere.

8. RUSH/URGENCY FEE

Urgent translations may necessitate a RUSH surcharge. As the time period required may not allow the time needed to perform the standard thorough quality control check, XYZ will not be liable for the standard of any work submitted on an urgent basis.

9. CANCELLATION

All orders are final. Exceptions made at the sole discretion of XYZ Translations, in the event of which the Client shall pay to XYZ 25% of the complete project cost or costs for the work completed, whichever is greater; costs for the work completed are based on the proportion of the complete fee that the completed work bears to the original text.

10. LIABILITY

a) When the fulfillment of obligations to the Client is prevented for any reason beyond XYZ's control, XYZ shall be relieved of all liability.

b) XYZ shall not under any circumstances be liable to the Client or any third party for loss or damage of any kind, and the Client shall indemnify XYZ against all claims and demands upon XYZ for any loss or damage.

c) If any error or omission in the translation is identified, XYZ will correct the work.

d) For a translation intended for publication, XYZ will accept responsibility for any errors or omissions only if the galley proof is submitted to XYZ for a final check before printing. The Client will be responsible for checking all figures (numbers and graphics) and XYZ will not be responsible for any errors in the figures.

e) In the event the Client uses the translation for a purpose other than that originally indicated, the Client shall not be entitled to any compensation by XYZ, and the Client shall indemnify XYZ against any resulting loss.

11. COPYRIGHT, CONFIDENTIALITY and LIBEL

The Client warrants that the translation does not infringe any copyright or other proprietary right and is not a betrayal of confidentiality or libel, and shall indemnify XYZ for all actions, claims, proceedings, costs and damages incurred or awarded and paid in respect of, or arising out of, any breach of such warranty or out of any claim by a thirdparty based on any facts that if sustained would constitute a breach of such warranty.

12. REPRESENTATION
An oral representation or statement shall not be binding upon XYZ, and nothing shall be implied from any such representation or statement.

13. COPYRIGHT
The Copyright of the translation is the property of XYZ, and becomes the Client's property only after receipt of full payment for the translation.

14. COMPLAINTS
Any complaint regarding the translation will be considered within 30 days of the date of translation delivery.

15. SETTLEMENT OF DISPUTES
The parties agree to make good faith efforts to settle disputes. Late payments will be assessed a penalty of 1.5% per month. Costs of collection efforts including but not limited to collection agency fees and/or attorney fees incurred during the collection process will be the responsibility of the Client. All disputes shall be brought within the territorial jurisdiction of (State you live).

16. GOVERNING LAW
All contractual relationships between the Client and XYZ shall be governed by United States law.

XYZ Signature & Name

_____

Client Signature, Name & Date

_____

Translation Client/Service Agreement Samples

Date of this Agreement: _____

John Smith ("Translator")

and _____ of _____("Client")

  Client's Name   Client's Address

Hereby agree as follows:

Description of services: Translator, as an independent contractor, will provide the following service(s) [Identify item(s) to be translated and the particular service(s) to be performed]:

_____

_____

_____

Scheduled completion date is: _____

Translator shall make every effort to complete service(s) by the above date but shall not be responsible for delays in completion caused by events beyond Translator's control.

Method of delivery: _____

Format of delivery: _____

Fee for services. Client agrees to pay $ _____ as Translator's fee for the above service(s). Payment is due as follows:

_____

_____

The due dates for payment of fees and costs under this Agreement shall be the date(s) specified in this Agreement, provided that if no date is specified, the due date shall be the date of Translator's billing for the fees or costs. Any payments for fees or costs not received by Translator within _____ days of the due date will be deemed late and shall

be subject to a _____% per month late charge. Client agrees to be responsible for Translator's costs in collecting late payments due from Client, including reasonable attorneys' fees.

Cancellation or withdrawal by Client: If Client cancels or withdraws any portion of the item(s) described in paragraph 1 above prior to Translator's completion of the service(s), then, in consideration of Translator's scheduling and/or performing said service(s) Client shall pay Translator the portion of the above fee represented by the percentage of total service(s) performed, but in any event not less than _____% of said fee.

Additional fees will be payable, to be calculated as provided below, in the event the following additional services are required: (a) investigation, inquiry, or research beyond that normal to a routine translation is required because of ambiguities in the item(s) to be translated; (b) additional services are required because Client makes changes in the item(s) to be translated after the signing of this Agreement; and (c) Translator is requested to make changes in the translation after delivery of the translation, because of Client's preferences as to style or vocabulary, and such changes are not required for accuracy. Such additional fees will be calculated as follows:

Additional costs: Client shall reimburse Translator for necessary out-of-pocket expenses incurred by

Translator that are not a normal part of routine translation procedure, such as overnight document delivery service requested by Client, long distance telephone and telefax expenses to clarify document ambiguity, etc.

Client's review of translation: Upon receipt of the translation from Translator, Client shall promptly review it, and within 30 days after receipt shall notify Translator of any requested corrections or changes. Translator shall correct, at no cost to Client, any errors made by Translator.

Confidentiality: All knowledge and information expressly identified by Client in writing as confidential which Translator acquires during the term of this Agreement regarding the business and products of Client shall be maintained in confidentiality by Translator and, except as expressly authorized by Client in writing, shall not be divulged or published by Translator and shall not be authorized by Translator to be divulged or published by others. **Confidential information for purposes of this paragraph shall not include the following:**
Information which is or becomes available to the general public provided the disclosure of such information did not result from a breach by Translator of this paragraph.

Terminological glossary entries compiled by Translator in the course of Translator's performance of the translation service(s) under this Agreement; provided, however, that Client and Translator may agree in writing that, upon payment by Client to Translator of an agreed-upon fee, such terminological glossary entries shall be the property of Client and shall be covered by the confidentiality provisions of this paragraph.

Translation is property of client, copyright. Upon Client's completion of all payments provided herein, the translation of the item(s) described in paragraph 1 above shall be the property of Client. Translator has no obligation to take any steps to protect any copyright, trademark or other right of Client with respect to the translation, except as may be expressly otherwise provided in this Agreement. Notwithstanding the foregoing, Translator shall have the right to retain file copies of the item(s) to be translated and of the translation, subject to the provisions of paragraph 7 above.

Indemnification and hold-harmless by Client: Client agrees to indemnify and hold Translator harmless from any and all losses, claims, damages, expenses or liabilities (including reasonable attorneys' fees) which Translator may incur based on information, representations, reports, data or product specifications furnished, prepared or approved by Client for use by Translator in the work performed under this Agreement.

Changes by others: Translator shall have no responsibility whatever as to any changes in the translation made by persons other than Translator.

Governing law: This Agreement shall be governed by the laws of the State of Indiana (Check your local state laws).

Additional provisions: [Add all additional provisions required by the parties.]

_____

_____

_____

Complete agreement: This is the complete agreement of the parties as to the subject matter hereof. Any changes in this Agreement must be in writing signed by both parties. This Agreement becomes a binding contract only upon signature by both parties and the delivery of fully signed copies to each party.

Translator: _____

Client: _____

Model Agreement for Translation Services

Translator

_____

Address

_____

Phone

_____

Pager

_____

Fax

_____

Social Security/

Tax I.D

_____

Client/And Company

_____

Address

_____

Phone

_____

Fax

_____

Agree to the following:

Service

Translator shall provide

Source/Target

Language

translation   narration   editing/proofreading

from _____   into _____

of the following document(s)

Brief Description

_____

_____

_____

_____

Due Date

Translator shall provide the above translation by

_____ provided that the project is received by

_____.

Translator shall deliver translation

Method of Delivery

by modem   by fax   by mail   by courier

Format

electronically, saved as_____

Fee

Client shall pay translator

at the rate of _____ per 100 source/target words.

at the rate of _____ per hour.

the fixed sum of _____.

Terms of Payment

Payment is due within _____ days of date of invoice.

Ownership

The source and target language materials do not become the property of the translator, but the translator has the right to retain file copies of the materials upon completion of the work.

Confidentiality

7. All knowledge and information acquired during the term of this Agreement with respect to the business and products of the client will be treated by translator as confidential until and unless stipulated by client.

Certification, DTP,
Metric Conversions,
Reimbursement of
Expenses etc.

8. Other agreed upon conditions and/or services:

_____

_____

_____

9. This agreement can be modified orally or in writing by agreement of both parties.

Signatures:

Approved and Accepted:

Client Signature/Date

_____

Translator Signature/
Date

_____

_____

_____

Model Agreement for Interpreter Services

Interpreter   _____

Address   _____

Phone   _____

Pager   _____

Fax   _____

Social Security   _____

And

Client/Company   _____

Address   _____

_____

Phone   _____

Fax   _____

agree to the following:

Service   Interpreter shall provide

simultaneous   consecutive   escort   interpreting

Languages   from and into   _____

for the following assignment:

Brief Description _____
Location

Address _____

Date _____

Time _____

Estimated Length
of Assignment _____
hours   days

Fee Client shall pay interpreter at the rate of _____ per hour
per ½ day
The fixed sum of _____.

Travel/mileage from _____ to assignment site
based on a fee schedule of _____
_____

Minimum fee of _____ if assignment is less than _____
hours.

Cancellation fee of _____ if assignment is canceled with less
than _____ hour notice.

No-show fee of _____ if assignment is canceled after
Interpreter is underway or has arrived at the assignment site.

Terms of Payment Payment is due within _____ days of date of invoice.

Confidentiality All knowledge and information acquired during this assignment
will be treated as confidential and that interpreter will adhere to
standard Interpreters Code of Ethics for this type of assignment.

Other Services   Other agreed upon conditions and/or services:

_____

_____

_____

This agreement can be modified orally or in writing by agreement of both parties.

Signatures: Approved and Accepted:

Client Signature/   _____
Date   _____

Interpreter   _____
Signature/Date   _____

For Discussion

You might want to consider drafting policies and procedures to cover the following scenarios:

1. What if the client (agency or end client) deems a translation *unsatisfactory*?

2. What if the translator delivers the project late (or never) and the client suffers damages?

3. What if the interpreter arrives late (or never) for an interpreting assignment and the client suffers damages?

4. What if the translator (or interpreter) accepts an offer to do freelance work for the end client without permission of the agency who introduced the translator (or interpreter) to the end client?

5. Prepayment/ half down payment sample

6. Rules regarding disputes

7. Reciprocal Non-compete agreement

8. Anti-poaching

9. How the Independent contractor is paid when, how (cash, check, etc.) for what, and what is not billable (reviewing your own work, mileage in-city, etc.)?

Tips for Negotiating Contracts

For the past fifteen years I have been primarily placed in management roles. A good percentage of my daily work involves the negotiation, interpretation and enforcement of contracts. While I enjoy all of the work, I have found that I get the most pleasure out of successfully negotiating contracts that are mutually beneficial to all the parties involved. Because the contracts form the basis for an ongoing relationship, I feel that it is imperative that much thought and planning go into the negotiation and execution of a contract. For these reasons, I would like to share with you some of the practices that I have developed over the past few years to help make negotiations go smoothly.

Your Negotiation Team

Before the first negotiation session, it is important to identify all of the individuals that may be necessary or helpful in creating a completed agreement. Attorneys, accountants, owners, managers and, sometimes, employees can all have a role to play in a successful negotiation. While the role of attorneys and accountants is somewhat obvious, less obvious may be the use of managers and employees. However, these individuals may have information about products, services or operations that could be of significance in the final contract. Because of this, some concern should be given to creating a negotiation team.

Preparation

All the members of a negotiation team should spend a significant amount of time preparing prior to the first meeting between the prospective parties. Any proposed contracts should be reviewed by all of the team members. Additional information about the other side may be gleaned from financial statements, court filings, and interviews with other customers or vendors. I have also found that that the Internet can be a rich source of background information.

While this initial preparation need not be overly exhaustive, information may be uncovered that alerts you to potential problems before the negotiations begin. This could result in terminating the negotiations before they have commenced, saving you significant time and money. A meeting or meetings between all of the team members will help keep the team on track and should avoid duplication of efforts. It should be the team's goal during this preparation phase to create a list of key issues.

The Key Issues

The careful identification of the key issues will play a vital role in the ultimate success or failure in reaching an agreement with the other party. Because the issues will vary from situation to situation, there is no boilerplate "list" which covers all the key issues that might arise in a given transaction. That is why it is imperative that each team member play an active role in identifying those issues that will be vital to the successful completion of the negotiation process.

Once the issues have been identified, some thought should be given to the order in which the issues should be raised with the other party and any negotiation strategies that may be employed. In developing strategies it is often helpful to role-play and put yourself and your team members in the other side's shoes.

Meeting the Other Side

While completed agreements are rarely reached at the first negotiation session, the tone set at the first meeting can be crucial in the ultimate success or failure of the process. Because of the importance of the first meeting, several "rules" should be followed.

First, the parties' respective negotiating teams should all be present. If the transaction is large enough, the parties may wish to meet informally the night before the actual negotiations begin. Because the principal negotiators do not always hold the keys to success, an informal dinner may allow the respective team members to form bonds, which will help smooth out the negotiation process.

The first meeting should be limited to the key issues already identified by the team members. The other side should be advised that your goal in approaching this first meeting is to determine whether further discussion of any "minor" issues is warranted. Neither side is served by undergoing a lengthy and difficult negotiation process only to see it eventually fail because a key issue was not raised early in the proceedings.

During the meeting, attempts to anticipate and discuss the needs of the other party and propose ways to address those needs and concerns while simultaneously meeting your own needs should be made. This will let the other side know that you recognize their issues and that you hope to be able to work toward a mutually beneficial conclusion.

Finally, the parties should take the time and effort to reach at least a conceptual agreement on the main issues before concluding the first meeting. In order to meet this goal, each of the team members should make sure that they have cleared their calendars in order to allow them to be present for the entire meeting. If the meeting is out of town, travel and accommodations should be arranged so that no one feels pressured because of flight departures or lodging restrictions.

The Site of the Negotiations

Prior to the first negotiation session, it is imperative that one party or the other takes responsibility for arranging appropriate facilities. While some negotiators may push to have the negotiations take place on a "home field" this should not be a major concern. Of concern should be the respective size of the negotiating teams and their representatives (attorneys, accountants etc.) and whether the facility is large enough to handle the members. Similarly, some principal players may not be able to travel or their schedules may be so busy that a location close to their office may allow them to be present for more of the negotiating session. Some concern should be made regarding meals and lodging if the negotiations may be lengthy. Will lunch be catered? Are there restaurants nearby?

Reaching a Conclusion IS Forming a Relationship

In addition to an adequate and thorough preparation; a successful result is more likely if all the participants keep in mind that the resulting contract between the parties will create an ongoing relationship. Because the relationship will be ongoing, the parties should, throughout the negotiation process, work to achieve clear and realistic expectations of what the other side will bring to and derive from the relationship.

Difficult and Sensitive Issues

Difficult and sensitive issues should be raised and discussed throughout the negotiation process. This will enable all the parties to form realistic expectations about how the proposed relationship will work. Unrealistic expectations often result in unsatisfactory relationships. Unsatisfactory relationships often result in disappointment and legal disputes.

Avoid Premature Position Taking

Before taking a particular position, it is often better to discuss each side's respective needs and interests. By adopting a discussion mindset as opposed to a position mindset the parties will become joint problem solvers rather than entrenched advisories. It is especially important to avoid ultimatums.

Ultimatums such as, "Unless you concede on that issue, we will terminate negotiations immediately" should be avoided. If an ultimatum is to be given, it should only be done so after all team members have had an opportunity to review and discuss it. Furthermore, the team must be prepared to back up its ultimatum.

Remain Flexible

Creativity will overcome many obstacles to reaching a successful conclusion. Remember that all the parties involved in the negotiation process have devoted much time, energy, effort and money in the hopes of reaching a satisfactory conclusion. Hopefully all of the parties will work together in an attempt to understand each side's respective concerns and reach solutions to those concerns. Rigid and inflexible positions will hinder discussion and squelch creativity.

Maintain Composure

Negotiations are often complex and frustrating. It is not uncommon for parties to have "highs" and "lows" during the negotiation process. It is important for all team members to recognize this fact and to remain composed, unemotional and in control at all times. Sarcastic or offhand remarks, sometimes made during tense periods, can slip out and do considerable harm to the negotiation process. Similarly, personal attacks or remarks about character should also be avoided. In addition to disrupting, and perhaps even sabotaging the negotiations, sarcastic comments and personal attacks can resurface even after successful negotiations and taint the ongoing relationship.

Remember Your Strength

Entering into negotiations does not bind two parties together. Either party can, theoretically, walk away at any time. While this "negotiation leverage" is held by both parties, it is important to not give it away at any time during the negotiation process. Be especially wary of offhand remarks that may alert the other side to a vulnerability or weakness relationship or business in your position.

Closing the Deal

Negotiations of major importance appropriately take a considerable amount of time. After the initial meeting, there may be several phone calls, letters, conversations and, hopefully, the discussion of proposed contracts. At some point, however, it will become important for one side or the other (or both) to either execute a final agreement or terminate the deal. Often times there may be two or three major issues left unresolved. To reach a resolution of these issues it is often wise to arrange another face to face meeting between all the team members. This time, however, the ground rules will be more strict in that each side should commit to remain together until (1) all of the remaining issues are resolved and the agreement is finalized for execution or (2) it is determined that an agreement cannot be reached and the negotiations should then be terminated.

Conclusion

While it may feel like it, a final contract is not a conclusion.   A contract merely marks the beginning of a formal relationship that may last for many years. By following the suggestions of this article, the relationship should begin in an open, honest and mutually beneficial way.

"Quality means doing it right when no one is looking."

— **Henry Ford**
Founder-Ford Motor Company

Chapter 17
QUALITY & ACCURACY
Dotting the I's and Crossing the T's

In the language industry you really are only as good as the quality of your work. If you contract out all of your projects then you are only as good as the quality of their work. But the key thing to remember before sending off any final product is proof, proof, proof.

When a client pays you for a translation they are paying for it to be accurate. You need to put a proofing system in place that isn't going to cost you a fortune but also isn't going to be so relaxed that you lose money from inaccurate translations.

Quality Control Processes

Quality Control (QC)

You may want to conduct random quality checks of the work submitted by your contractors for your clients to ensure they are happy with the service and that the projects are being carried out correctly and accurately. It's also a good way to keep up on the quality of your translation teams and contractors. If you do run into a potential problem remember these words of wisdom, "I'll look into it."

The client isn't always right and neither are you. When I first started I assumed the client was right and did not charge for any discrepancies on a project and I lost a lot of money from it. Whether you are wrong or right is less important than how will the problem be fixed? It's in your best interest to fix the problem and get back to the client as soon as possible. If it's a problem with a specific translator, simply don't use them anymore. They aren't employees of yours so no one is getting fired or let go, you just don't need their service anymore. Use the following methods to ensure projects are being completed accurately and on time:

Translation Teams

A translation team is a group of people with a full set of complementary skills required to complete a translation task, job, or project. This type of team is usually assembled when the translation project is large, complex and/or has many facets to the overall project.

Proofreading

Proof reader will review translation projects for accuracy and consistency and proof the copy of a text in order to detect and correct any errors

Translation Memory Software

Translation memory software, or TM, is a database that stores segments that have been previously translated. A translation-memory system stores the words, phrases and paragraphs that have already been translated and aid human translators. The translation memory stores the source text and its corresponding translation in language pairs called "translation units".

I have included a flow chart for both translation and interpreting projects on the following pages.

LANGUAGE TRANSLATION PROJECT CYCLE/PHASES

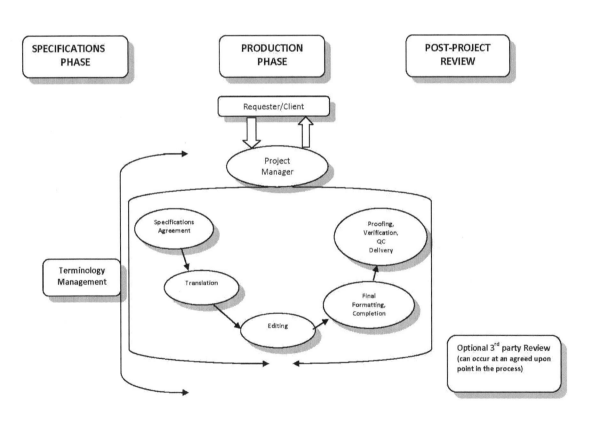

INTERPRETING PROJECT
CYCLE/PHASES

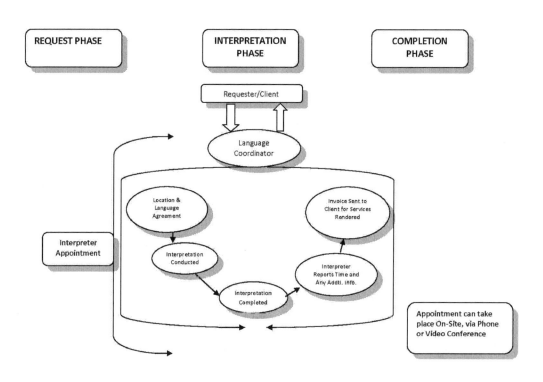

ISO 9001:2000 Certification

The International Organization for Standardization (ISO) is a network of the national standards institutes of 147 countries. ISO is used by over 300,000 companies worldwide. With a central secretariat in Geneva, Switzerland, the ISO sets rigorous standards for business, government, and industry.

A translation or interpreting company that has ISO 9001:2000 Certification has achieved the highest level of quality assurance. Although companies that are ISO certified usually charge more, the credibility and confidence that go along with using this type of agency is priceless.

Additional Quality Assurance Check

One way in which you are able to improve your translation processes in order to obtain close to optimal quality results over all of your translations, all the while keeping costs low, is through implementation of an additional quality assurance check at the end of every translation and/or localization project.

Final Quality Assurance Check

No one is perfect and even the best translators can make small mistakes sometimes. However, in order to eliminate such instances and keep such variances to a minimum, you should add a "Final Quality Assurance Check," so as to create and maintain consistently error-free translations. This Final Quality Check usually takes place after you send the completed translation to the client and they have inserted the translated text into the program, software or file they will be using to print the project.

Have your clients send you projects before they print them. On occasions the software at the printing company can have an impact on the translation- omitting accent marks, not recognizing characters and replacing fonts with incorrect fonts or images. By adding this check, you will be able to lower costs for all parties (i.e. revision costs, additional per hour charges for further translations, opportunity costs and time to completion) and increase quality while offering services at attractive prices.

"The way a team plays as a whole determines its success. You may have the greatest bunch of individual stars in the world, but if they don't play together, the club won't be worth a dime."

— **Babe Ruth**
NY Yankees

Chapter 18
PERSONNEL & HR ISSUES
Let Me Introduce You to My Staff

In the beginning it will be simple and sweet. The only employee you may need is yourself. When you are initially starting the company it will probably be best just to have yourself on board to save on costs. Keep in mind that this means you are in charge of all scheduling, client interaction, recordkeeping and in-house translating/ word processing for your company, as well as serving as the sales representative for your services.

If you find that down the road that you need to hire more personnel due to your work load that's okay. Just remember that the more you can do by yourself the better because you don't have to pay someone to do work you could do on your own. Depending on your work load and the amount of projects you choose to accept will give you a good idea of how many employees to hire.

As your business grows you may need to hire an administrative assistant, office manager, language/project director, sales reps, financial manger/bookkeeper, and possibly additional translators.

Hiring an administrative assistant will cut back on work that seems minor when you have more stuff to do. Answering the phone and taking messages for you will save you more time than you actually realize. They will also be handling a majority of the mail and other incoming and outgoing information like bills and faxes. It's a good idea, although not a necessity, to hire someone that is bilingual.

This person does not need to have a degree but it is a good idea that they have basic computer skills and pleasant manners. If they are not a full time employee you should pay them hourly and not salary. Depending on their work load and tasks that you have your administrative assistant will depend on what you choose to pay them. Check your local SBA or Chamber of Commerce for average rates and fees for staff.

Keeping organized is part of running a smooth and worry free business. Keeping everything in order requires constant attention when you are busy so it's not a bad idea to hire an office manager to keep everything in line for you if you have a heavy work load. Office managers can be responsible for hiring, scheduling and also bookkeeping. The first thing you will need them to do is to establish a filing system if you don't already have one in order. This will be an easy way to keep track of all accounts and companies records as well as billing and employee information.

An office manager will also oversee many of the daily operations of the office and act as a boss unofficially. They will perform employee evaluations and make sure everything is running smooth around the office. In doing all of this they could fill in for you when you aren't there to "crack the whip."

Depending on the size of your company you may need to hire a professional bookkeeper to maintain order throughout all of your accounts. However, there are many types of software programs currently available that make doing your own books quick and simple like QUICKBOOKS. Most software programs range from $200 to $500 which may seem like a large cost initially, but just think about all the money it saves you from hiring someone to do your bookkeeping for you. When drawing up our budget we figured in about $250 a month for bookkeeping services. Before hiring anyone, ask yourself if you truly need them. If you don't need someone there to help out and it's something you can do on your own, don't hire them.

Visit your local bookstore or library to read more about HR issues and hiring employees. You can also talk to a friend or someone you know that's in human resources about hiring people. They will be able to give you lots of tips and tricks into picking out the right people to work with. Keep in mind that each person is unique and different and you only get them for eight hours of the day. That means sixteen hours a day they have things other than work going on in their life.

I learned a huge lesson with the first group I hired. I had someone working for me that had managed to find a loophole in every employee policy that I had, or in this case, every policy I didn't have in place. I had no policy on showing up late or taking days off without prior notice. I was too much of a nice guy back then. The man working for me used each and every excuse to get out of work including having jury duty about one day every week. When I finally asked for a slip for jury duty, the days off were put to a halt.

I learned very quickly to make up new rules and rules for those rules. When designing a handbook or a list of rules for employees plan for the worst so that you don't hear "well I don't know what your policy is on that." It's a good idea to talk to someone in human resources about what thoughts they may have.

"Advertising is legalized lying"

- **H.G. Wells**
Author, *The War of the Worlds*

Chapter 19
MARKETING 101

Marketing Your Hot New Business

___

Marketing Basics

Marketing is the life blood of all businesses. What you will find is that marketing includes several areas that may overlap from time to time. You will discover that no matter how great the marketing, if the placement, price or timing is off your marketing efforts will ultimately fail. Here are some basic areas that should be addressed when creating your basic marketing plan.

Naming your business

What seems to be the most fun can turn into the most technical. Picking a name for your company is not as simple as deciding it and putting up a sign. The name of your business can either make or break you. Ideally your name should convey the expertise, value and uniqueness of the services you've developed.

Choose several names that you like and then try them out on sample groups like friends and family. Be sure to check state and local requirements to assure that you aren't stepping on another business' toes which can put you in hot water legally. Once you do decide on a name for your company you can secure it by going to your state's Secretary of State Office. To broaden your advances, also check in with the U.S. Patent and Trademark Offices.

I've come across books and websites that help some but honestly if you want to go big with the marketing and advertising, your best bet is to go with a marketing agency. The only problem is that once they develop a marketing plan for you, even if you choose to go another route, you still pay for that plan.

Below is an example of a Marketing Plan that will help you target or segment the market you are trying to reach. I know you would like to get all the translation business in the world. However, it will be easier and smarter to try and reach those people needing Spanish translation services in a 20-mile radius of your target area and so on. Your job will be to find out who these potential clients are, what is their age, profession, sex and other information that will help you in placing your message where it will be seen by the largest segment of your target audience as often as possible, also known as "Penetration" at the lowest cost to you.

The **Small Business Administration's** website offers a "Marketing your business for success" online plan.

Elements of a Marketing Plan

Description of Target Market

- Age
- Sex
- Profession
- Income level
- Educational level
- Residence

Description of Competitors

- Market research data
- Demand for product or service
- Nearest direct and indirect competitors
- Strengths and weaknesses of competitors
- Assessment of how competitors businesses are doing
- Description of the unique features of your product or service
- Similarities and differences between your service and competitors

Description of Service

- Describe your service
- Emphasize special features, ex) your selling points

Marketing Budget

- Advertising and promotional plan
- Cost estimated for advertising and promotions
- Advertising and promotional materials
- List of advertising media to be used and an estimate of cost for each medium used

Description of Location

- Description of the location
- Advantages and disadvantages of location

Pricing Strategy

- Pricing techniques and brief description of these techniques
- Retail costing and pricing
- Competitive position
- Pricing below competition
- Pricing above competition
- Price lining
- Multiple pricing
- Service components
- Material costs
- Labor costs

Websites

Business Website(s)

More than 100 million people use the Internet each day. A website is one of the most effective ways to market your small business. Your website can help get the word out immediately about a project or product, level the playing field for small businesses that compete with big businesses. It can enable small business to expand their business nationally or internationally. Since launching my businesses website 10 years ago 50% of my business has been conducted online.

Website Basics

A good website shows by doing; it proves rather than states. Instead of making claims, it provides evidence.

Evidence:
- Case Studies showing how your efforts solved a previous client's problems.

- Testimonials from satisfied clients.

- Reprints of articles you've written or reviews of your work.

Education, however, remains the best way to establish credibility. To the extent prospects leave your website better informed about your product or service, the easier it is to gain their respect the faster you will gain their purchase order.

Three steps to creating your own business web site.

Today's tools make web publishing accessible to small business without programming experience. For example, Microsoft Office, Vista and Microsoft 7 all include a design assistant for web design elements and design templates to help your build a workable and respectable website.

Whether you build the site yourself or contract a designer or design company here are some steps to follow to ensure your website is a success.

Step one: Choose a structure and a look. Your site should be structured and designed to best tell your story. But where do you start? You can choose from pre-designed options that can later be customized so that establishing a structure and "look" is easy or take samples of websites you like to your designer.

Step two: Tell your story. Next, simply select the sample headlines and text provided and replace them with words that describe what you have to offer.

Step three: Check your work and post your site. Before you release your web address to the world make sure that all your links, videos and images are working properly.

Remember, with millions of websites, you may have to market your website as well as your small business to get traffic for your business. The website can be an inexpensive way of effectively building your small business. If you need to send out lots of emails (1,000+), companies like constant contact or icontact can help with templates, hosting and sending out your email marketing at a very low cost. If you try to send several email messages out from your personal email account they may be marked as SPAM and be placed directly in the receiver's junk mail box.

10 Tips for Website Online Marketing

1. Put up a simple web page.
2. Use a name that will attract people
3. Give away advice and information
4. Have lots of e-mail correspondence
5. Provide customized pages for users.
6. Visit users groups

7. Get on mailing lists
8. Arrange links with related sites
9. Make sure you're in every possible directory
10. Do not "SPAM"

Other Marketing Basics

- Business Card, Letterhead, etc.

- Logo

- Tagline (Ex. Burger King tagline: *"Have it Your Way"*)

- Email Account (Make sure your account can receive large email files)

- Brochure (8.5 x11)

SEO

What is SEO? Search engine optimization (SEO) is the process of improving the volume or quality of traffic to a web site from search engines via "natural" or un-paid ("organic" or "algorithmic") search results as opposed to search engine marketing (SEM) which deals with paid inclusion. Typically, the earlier (or higher) a site appears in the search results list, the more visitors it will receive from the search engine. SEO may target different kinds of search, including image search, local search, video search and industry-specific vertical search engines. This gives a web site web presence.

As an Internet marketing strategy, SEO considers how search engines work and what people search for. Optimizing a website primarily involves editing its content and HTML and associated coding to both increase its relevance to specific keywords and to remove barriers to the indexing activities of search engines. You can do the basic SEO optimizing of your website on your own. However, for high quality SEO optimization I encourage you to hire a professional when the time is right and you have money to invest in this service.

Tip

Use the business plan when purchasing and/or placing your advertising. There are also several books, websites and magazine articles on this topic. I encourage you to do your homework on this topic since it will be an ongoing cost and process for the life cycle of your business. Reaching your customers has never been as cheap and direct, with the creation of the internet, websites, online advertising and social networks it is now more affordable than ever before.

"It is better to be looked over than to be overlooked."

— **Mae West**
Actress

Chapter 20
IMAGE AND ETIQUETTE
Make a GREAT First Impression

Business Etiquette

Business etiquette is more than knowing which fork to pick up for your salad versus your entrée. Business etiquette is the way that you carry yourself and your ability to be comfortable in your own shoes. It is not arrogance, it is confidence and please do your best not to confuse the two because it is a very fine line and the last thing you want to do is be "that person."

Being in the translation business, you are almost certain to be dealing with people from other countries and it is a good idea to be familiar with main customs from their country. For example, in Japan, it is never appropriate for men to wear casual clothing to a business meeting and women's business attire must always be conservative and never showy.

Dress for success. It's a good idea to blend into your market, because you want to look good, but not stand out too much. Keep your attire in general solid colors of black, navy, or grey. Tan is also fine in the winter time. Don't try to be overly fashionable, just professional. You could be in a courtroom, classroom and doctors office all in the same day...you just never know.

Don't forget: a hand shake says a lot about a person. Don't intimidate your clients, but also be sure and show them you mean business.

Basic Wardrobe

Men: Dark suit—material matters, solid white or blue dress shirt underneath.

Silk ties that aren't too showy, no cartoon character or piano key ties please.

Make sure your socks are not only calf length and match your suit, but make sure they match each other. Guys you know you look at other guys shoes so make sure they are nice and conservative, clean and match your outfit well. Reminder: don't forget to match your belt to your shoes also. The best accessory if any to remember, good hygiene. Good breath and not too much cologne is a must when meeting with clients.

Women: You can't go wrong with a skirted suit or a pants suit. Make sure everything is tailored well to your body so it does not to look too sloppy and skirts are at a modest and conservative length. Tops can add color and variety to ordinary everyday outfits but be sure to not go extreme with necklines or patterns. Remember professional, not prostitute. It's common for women in the business world to wear hose with their attire and nude color not only hides pale legs and keeps you warmer in the winter, but it makes your legs look smooth and flawless as well.

Open toed shoes are not professional or usually allowed in many offices so save your high heeled party shoes for the evening and stick with a conservative low heel in a traditional black or brown color.

It is always better to be overdressed than underdressed. If you go to a business meeting and everyone else is dressed down it's easy for men to take off a suit jacket or a tie, but if you arrive and everyone else is dressed nicer than you are, you don't have much to work with.

Dining out

The first thing to place in order when meeting with someone is the location. Make sure that it is a place convenient for the other person and also a place where you won't be distracted. Lunch and dinner places will vary but make sure it's clear you are there for business.

If you have any literature or contracts that you and your client are discussing, make sure they have a copy of it a few days before the meeting so that they don't feel ambushed. This gives them the opportunity to go over all of the paper work and think things through clearly.

When planning out your meal out with a client, it's a good idea to ask if they will be bringing anyone else. You may need to discuss finances or other personal aspects of the deal you are working on and it may not be appropriate for someone else to be attending.

Once all of the preplanning for the meeting is mapped out in your head it's time for the actual event; the dinner meeting. Punctuality, Punctuality, Punctuality. I can't say it enough. If you show up late, you might as well not show up at all because you're showing them that their business is not important to you. In the case of an emergency you are to arrive late, it is okay. Just make sure that you call the restaurant and let them know so they can pass along the message.

It is still best to arrive before the client. This allows you to get settled, speak to your server and let them know it's a business meeting. Once your clients arrive they will know I'm sure, but this gives the server a heads up. Give them your credit card beforehand so that at the end of the meal there is no confusion about the check and the server simply brings you a slip to sign. It's a very suave move.

When your client arrives, give them the better seat. Don't sit them in a place they will be distracted by anything so all of their attention will be on you and the subject at hand. Their back to the door is usually best.

Take time to get to know them, unless you're on a tight schedule, don't jump right into business. Take a few moments to unwind. Build the relationship. When you get into the matter at hand, ask them what their needs are so that you have their best interest in mind.

When speaking to your client. Talk clearly and slowly. If you are a fast talker, slow it down because it will appear as if you are trying to rush through things.

Don't have unnecessarily long or multiple meetings, a lot can be done over the phone. So don't waste your time or theirs. If you want to meet with them just to go out, call a friend, not a client.

Tip

I meet primarily with CEO's and key decision makers of companies so that I do not waste my time and efforts. Be sure to find out who really makes decisions at the company you are trying to do business with. You may find that the CEO pays the bills but the Director of Marketing makes all the decisions about vendors. I have found that it is cheaper and less hectic to meet for coffee mid-day versus trying to schedule a 1-hour lunch.

Other Things to Consider

It's always good to keep a suit coat in your office or your car because you never know what the day will bring and you may have an important meeting with a client or somewhere else that requires a more dressed up look.

Always be prepared for TV or radio interviews. Some people aren't comfortable being on camera or public speaking, but keep in mind that it is free publicity and it establishes your credibility if you are putting yourself out in the community. Any good PR for your company is always great.

It doesn't matter whether you are male or female you will always face bias. The important thing to do is not take it personal; it's just business. Which is also why you should not bad mouth competition, it negatively affects your image and may come back to haunt you.

Nametag

Several clients request interpreters identify themselves, company they work for and the language they are fluent in on their nametag for convenience and safety purposes.

Ex. **JOHN DOE**
XYZ Interpreting
Japanese Interpreter

The whole process of getting started is a journey. You're going to face things that will come easier to some and more difficult to others. The thing to remember is not to give up.

"It's the start that stops most people."

*"We need to talk about
your TPS reports"*

— **Bill Lumbergh**
Office Space

Chapter 21
OPPORTUNITIES & CHALLENGES

The Bumps In The Road

Starting a new business is going to give you some challenges. There are a few things in which you should be aware of that I was not warned about when I started my business. It's so important to read up on the language and translation industry. Know the in's and the out's of your business and try to learn as much about the industry as you possibly can. It is also important to learn about the communication industry.

When starting a company, not matter who you are, you are going to face a number of problems. Many people are just set in their ways and have old ways of thinking. All of the, what I like to call "isms" will come into play at some point. (Ex. Ageism, Sexism, Racism, etc.)

When I started my company I was 24 years old so everyone thought that I was too young. No one wanted to invest in my business because they thought I was just some young guy. Women will face issues just because they are women, as well as people of different ethnicity. The important thing is not to let it get you down. Find a way to work around it or use it to your advantage. Someone is always going to be counting you out, but use that as motivation to show them that you mean business.

Admitting problems or potential issues from the start will save you a big headache in the long run. You also may be cleaning up messes that faulty translators have left behind which could potentially hurt your image in the beginning so make sure to take that into consideration. Keep the cash flow accurate because if someone isn't paying, then someone isn't getting paid, which could result in unhappy workers. It may be a good idea to have someone help with your billing and accounting if you have a large client base.

Time management is a challenge no matter what business you are in, especially if you are doing a lot of the translating yourself. Outsourcing may be the better option when it comes to managing your time because as a business owner, you'll be doing a lot more than just translating. You'll probably have meetings upon meetings with people from the community and business society.

In the beginning of your business volunteering on projects and for other translation companies can help you as an entry into the market so that you can get acquainted with the industry. The experience and networking that you gain is truly invaluable. You will really gain a concept of the whole industry by volunteering on projects that you may not have considered in the past. The people that you form relationships with now are those that you can turn to again in your career if you need help with something.

Your net worth is only as good as your network. This networking ability really can make opportunities endless. The more people you know, the more people that know you, and whenever they have a translation issue with their business they are coming straight to you.

Depending on your abilities, past experience, and education, opportunities will vary but they are all out there. If you have the language ability you can do it yourself or even partner with other companies. I've never been a big fan of becoming a middle man but here's how I see it: the more you outsource, the more time you have to develop new ways to make money, and you can then justify your salary. If all you do is take someone's project and send it off to someone else, what are you really doing to deserve your paycheck at the end of the month?

Books and other publications are seeking translators to transform their works into something more universal. Keep in mind that these projects will take longer than others so be sure to inform your client of that. Website business is picking back up. There was a period of time when websites had slowed down their website translation requests, but they are back on the rise and eager to make their web pages accessible to the world.

Translation opportunities are endless with so many different projects and legal documents that need to be translated. Birth certificates, death certificates, adoption licenses, divorce papers, and marriage licenses are all projects that are not only in high demand, but very essential to people in the community. You can't get married until you can prove that you're divorced.

Many companies are importing and exporting materials so you won't always just deal with translating things from English into another language, but frequently from another language back into English, which opens up and entire new industry.

From working in the translation industry, many people will also wonder if you do interpreting as well. This can open up many new doors for you if you choose to take that route. Courts and legal personnel are always in need of interpreters as well as people in the medical field. The interpretation industry is growing just as fast as the translation industry.

Your image is one of your best personal opportunities. If you make yourself presentable then people will more willing to deal with you. So glance back at the section on image and keep in mind little tricks like keeping a suit jacket in your car or a pair of heels for women. That way you will always be prepared.

Finally, one of the biggest challenges will be keeping talented contractors (interpreters, translators and designers) from going on their own, even if you have a signed non-compete agreement. Almost every person that has worked for me over the years has asked me for more money. There have been some contractors who just thought they would do work on the side for my clients and that I wouldn't find out. I quickly reprimanded both the contractor and the client, telling each that if they did not want to work with me or for my business then we would stop working with them immediately. What people realize is that a short term benefit is not worth a long time loss in money and/or services.

In the following chapter I will go into more detail on when to bring in the lawyers to solve concerns and problems. Like it or not, once you go into business the likely hood that you will be sued or that you will have to bring a lawsuit upon someone greatly increase.

"To open a shop is easy, to keep it open is an art"

— Chinese Proverb

Chapter 22
PROTECTING YOUR (ASS)ET'S

When Times are Tough Buy a Helmet

Recession

Business or economic cycles fluctuate in the United States from a macroeconomics perspective, entering the business world subjects you to going with the flow of the business cycle. This could be really good in some cases, or pretty awful like the recession of 2008/2010. What is a recession?

During a recession, the economy is the dark period right before a country hits a depression. This is caused by decline in the country's GDP (gross domestic product) or negative economic growth for two or more successive quarters of the year. This may have an impact on the business cycle and may cause even more obstacles when it comes to borrowing from lenders who may be hesitant to lend money when the economy is not doing well. This just means that you have to prove even more that you deserve the loan over someone else. It's a good idea to stress that opening your business may soon provide jobs for people in the community; this is something the banks and lenders look at closely.

A recession will also mean that some businesses will go out of business and some just can't pay their bills. Make sure to at least get a 50% on big projects so you're not left with a loss because a client had to shut down their business. If a client is having trouble paying you it is best to try to work out a payment plan at the very least, small payments are better than no payments.

General Payment Terms

Terms

General payment terms are 30-45 days up to 60-90 days on some projects. What this means is that it could take a client at least 1 month from the time you invoice them to pay you for the project. You will have to float the costs you incurred to complete the project for the same amount of time. This has always caused confusion for contractors that are waiting to get paid for projects they completed for you since some think you already got paid or that you are the end-client.

Make sure you are clear with contractors and vendors when and how they will be paid (Ex. Contractor will be paid by check within 15-days of payment by client. The payment will be sent via standard mail). This will reduce or eliminate the number of contractors calling or coming to your office demanding immediate payment in cash. Yes. It has happened.

I do not advise you to pay for projects that you haven't been paid for yet since there may be a reason you haven't been paid. There could be a problem with the project and the work completed by the contractor, inaccurate reporting of time by contractor and other billing or quality issues that could impact when or if the project will be paid for. If you start paying for projects you have not been paid for, you could end up with everyone being paid except you if something goes wrong. The once profitable project has now put you in the poor house or bankrupt especially if the project and/or loss is substantial. Make sure the 50% deposit you request at the on-set of a large project (usually anything over $500-$1,000) will cover your contractor and material costs in case the client cannot pay the remaining portion of your fees, this will ensure you at least break-even.

Understanding Business Cycles

Business trends seem to be the same across the board no matter what industry you are in. The first three months of the year make up the 1st quarter. In the beginning months of the calendar year, many people go to work on projects that they put off towards the end of the previous year. This makes for higher reported earnings for the first quarter of the year.

It is best not to get too ahead of yourself because next comes the 2nd quarter. Because most people either do so much work in the 1st quarter, or get too ahead of themselves, the 2nd quarter usually doesn't produce a great amount of activity so it's almost certain that you won't receive as much profit 2nd quarter as you did in the 1st. During the third quarter people usually get back on their feet and decide to invest in projects or revisit projects they put on the back burner that they didn't get around to in the 2nd quarter.

The 4th quarter (usually the end of the calendar year) is tricky, you may have a client that has excess funds in their marketing budget that they must spend or you may have no work at all. However, on average little to no activity goes on during the 4th quarter much like how it's the worse time to quit your job because no one is ever hiring during the holidays. Many people are so consumed with the holiday season that no work really gets done. So to sum it up simply: 1st and 3rd quarters = good workloads, 2nd and 4th quarters= minimal workloads.

The best time to have your business up and running would be the start of 1ˢᵗ quarter. With the new year comes your new business and you're up and running as soon as your New Year's Eve party clean up is finished. Start to get things ready to go towards the end of the year, around fall, this will give you the final few months of the year to get everything around and organized so you can launch in January. Plus starting at the beginning of the year gives you an entire year before you have to start messing with taxes. Not a bad reason for holding off right?

Protecting you ASSet's & Interests

I am not a big fan of lawyers or problems but you will run into both along the way, especially if a business cycle or recession impacts your client's ability to pay you. Another reason you will have problems or have to call upon the services of a lawyer is theft. The stealing of clients, information, equipment and/or money will be reason to pursue legal action. It could be the contractor that has worked for you the longest, a competitor, a family member, a close friend or your largest vendor, you just never know who is going to steal from you and when. In this chapter I will lay out some basic strategies to protect your ASSets and interests.

Protecting Your Rates & Client List

Every week I get someone calling in asking me for my rates pretending to be a client. I tell them what I would tell a "real" potential client, *"I need to see the project. There are several factors that go into our rates so the best way to get an accurate quote is to let us get a look at the project."* Some people will still ask if I could just give them a ballpark figure, which I do, and I usually don't hear back from the person.

This is good for me and usually bad for the other person since they will probably use the figure I give them, that figure did not take into account several factors (see Ch.13 What to Charge For..?) and after a few projects that take forever with little to no profit the person or "competitor" will drop out of the language industry. This is also the reason why I generally do not release a list of my clients, if someone wants to know who I have done work for I give them a list of project types and industries I have provided services for.

My rates also are watermarked with the words "CONFIDENTIAL," in case I have to take the person or business to court later for using my rates to bid on projects or worse, using my rates to steal my clients.

Non-Compete Clauses & Agreements

There have been only two occasions that I did not have an employee or contractor sign a non-compete agreement and I have regretted each to this day. I don't care who the person is or for how long you have known them, make everyone sign a non-compete. What is a non-compete? A non-compete agreement/clause or covenant not to compete (CNC), is a term used in contract law under which one party (usually an employee or contractor) agrees not to pursue a similar profession or trade in competition against another party (usually the employer).

The use of such clauses and agreements is used to prevent the employee or contractor who upon their termination or resignation, might begin working for a competitor or starting a business, and gain competitive advantage by abusing confidential information about their former employer's operations or trade secrets, or sensitive information such as customer/client lists, business practices, upcoming products, and marketing plans.

Additionally, a business might abuse a non-compete clause or agreement to prevent an employee from working elsewhere at all. Most jurisdictions in which such contracts have been examined by the courts have deemed CNCs to be legally binding so long as the clause contains reasonable limitations as to the geographical area and time period in which an employee of a company may not compete. Courts have held that, as a matter of public policy, an individual cannot be barred from carrying out a trade in which (s)he has been trained except to the extent that is necessary to protect the employer.

The extent to which non-compete clauses are legally allowed varies per jurisdiction. Some jurisdictions, such as the state of California, invalidate non-compete-clauses for all but equity stakeholders in businesses.

*DeSoto Representatives: Please visit the DeSoto website, (www.DESOTOTRANSLATIONS.com) for downloadable- Ready-To-Use Agreements and Contracts.

Service Agreements for Clients

This agreement is something I use with vendors primarily to outline my terms and responsibilities for both client & provider (you). This is also where you may want to include other provisions like payment terms (50% deposit), Preferred Rates & Discounts, Confidentiality clause and anti-poaching clause.

Anti-poaching & Confidentiality Clauses

These two clauses are very important in the language industry because you will be providing services to various industries and agencies. One thing I have run into over the years is clients using my rates to negotiate better contracts with competitors and directly approaching my contractors ("Poaching") to contract directly with the client. It never ceases to amaze me the crazy things people will do. Protect yourself at the beginning of your business from this type of threat. *I advise you to include terms or statements for the two clauses above in all your agreements.

Firing Clients

From time to time you will have a client that does not follow your businesses policies, procedures or is just such a pain you don't want to work with them. If your business is structure as a for-profit entity you can easily remedy this problem. Stop working with this client. If you are set up as a not-for-profit you will need to create a policy regarding when and how you deny services to these types of clients. There are also rude, disrespectful and intimidating clients that no person should have to put up with. If at any time you feel that the client is violating your policies, procedures (demanding service same-day without prior arrangements, working past agreed time/hours, etc.) you should have a plan of action to address these actions. Example: Initial Warning, written warning, cancellation of account/ services, leaving location immediately, etc. Whatever your policy it should be in writing and your clients should be aware of them as well.

Firing Contractors (Poor Work, Unethical Practices, "Competition" After-hours, etc.)

There will be contractors that inevitably do not work out for several reasons. The most common reason is poor work performance. Second common reason for "firing" contractors is that they are constantly tardy to appointments. The third most common reason to stop working with a contractor (interpreter, translator, etc.) is that they violate their non-compete agreement they signed with you by providing services after-hours to various client's, or worse yet, your current clients. The easiest way to "fire" a contractor is to stop using them.

Make sure you send a letter informing the contractor that you will not be using their services in the future; you do not need to give a reason in most cases, and that you will be enforcing the Non-Competition clause in the agreement they signed. If this does not stop the person from competing or soliciting your clients you will need to get your lawyer involved. ENFORCE THIS CLAUSE. If you do not enforce this clause you will become known as the person that can be taken advantage of, this is not a good distinction to have.

Firing Employee

If you are firing an actual employee you may need to refer to your employee handbook regarding terminations and reprimands. There needs to be a clear and fair policy and procedure for terminating employees. If you are just starting your business you can by pre-written employee handbook software or you can have a professional HR consultant draft a policy for you for a few hundred dollars. Either way you do it, you need to have a policy in place to prevent a lawsuit for unethical practices or for violating your employee's rights.

*DeSoto Representatives: Please visit the DeSoto website, (www.DESOTOTRANSLATIONS.com) for downloadable- Ready-To-Use Agreements and Contracts.

"*There is only one way... to get anybody to do anything. And that is by making the other person want to do it.*"

— **Dale Carnegie**
Author & Motivational Speaker

Chapter 23
WRITING & MAKING PROPOSALS
Sounds Good, Can You Send Me a Proposal?

Nobody enjoys doing it, but we've all had to do our fair share of writing speeches and making proposals for something or someone. Remember back in school when you'd stay up all night going over your speech just to forget it all the moment you stood in front of the class. Writing and making proposals can seem like torture but it's really not any different than when you were in school.

Keep in mind that a business proposal is not a business plan. Although you may be required to use some or most of the same information, the business proposal is what you will be providing potential clients as a bid for their business. So your main driving force behind the writing of the proposals is not to get money from a lender, it is to win over a potential customer. Be sure to bring into play that you have the clients best interests and needs in mind; this can be evident in the proposal if you really have no interest in pleasing your client and are solely focused on your needs and profits.

A winning business proposal requires optimal communication. Make sure you know the needs and wants of your client. I really cannot stress this enough. The client needs to see first and foremost that your solution or proposal is superior to all others that may come across their desk.

Proposal Writing Tips:

- Be sure to have an alluring cover letter. If they don't want to read past your cover letter you have wasted your time.

- Make sure your executive summary draws the reader in as well.

- Prove to the reader that you understand their entire list of wants and needs

- Propose your strategies for meeting their wants and needs along with your optimal solution and how it benefits them

- Include your company's unique selling position. What makes you better above all others?

- What is this going to cost the client?

- Significant issues and deadlines for projects to be completed and a brief explanation of the timing

- Leave them with something to secure the fact that you aren't giving them false expectations. Testimonials, reviews, references, and samples from other clients will help ensure your credibility.

- And finally; provide the reader with your most gripping request for the contractual agreement and business by doing everything short of getting on your knees and begging.

- Give them 2-3 options to choose from. Option 1, being the most inclusive and most expensive, Option 2, similar to Option 1 minus a few bells and whistles, and so on.

- Do your homework.

Basic Elements of a Proposal:

Summary: Clearly and concisely summarizes the request.

Introduction: Describes the agency's/organizations qualifications, history or credibility.

Problem: Documents the needs to be met or problems to be solved.

Objectives: Establishes the benefits of the proposal/solution in measurable terms.

Goals: Describes in detail the measurable terms (ex. 20 kids will graduate).

Methods: Describes the activities to be employed to achieve the desired results.

Evaluation: Presents a plan for determining the degree to which objectives are met and methods followed.

Future or Other Necessary Needs: Describes a plan for continuation beyond the initial proposal and/or other resources necessary to implement the project.

*Budget: Clearly delineates costs and resources need to complete or implement the proposal.

Important Considerations for a Well Written Proposal

The Proposal Should:

• State Who, What, When Where, Why and how much you're asking for in the first paragraph of your proposal and your letter of intent/interest.

• Be a well thought out plan. All costs should be listed.

• Follow logically from one idea to another. The entire proposal should be a logical and sequential argument.

• Have a positive tone.

- Be clear, concise and specific.

- Exclude Jargon, "Spanglish" or be written using bureaucratic lingo.

- Exclude big words or pompous phrases. Keep it simple.

- Exclude vague generalizations and promises.

- Minimal use of acronyms, unless absolutely necessary, and then provide explanations.

- Use simple sentences, keep paragraphs short (particularly the first two paragraphs of each section or sub-section), use headings and subheadings.

- Exclude unsupported assumptions.

- Have a combination of statements, statistics, and quotes and occasion, case examples. However, be careful, too many statistics may be boring and you increase the chance for errors.

- Client Driven: It should be written from the point of view of those who will benefit from the proposed program/project. This should include clients as well as other beneficiaries.

- Show the credibility of the applicant's credentials.

- Develop a system to quantify your proposals impact and success.

- Have someone outside the group working on the proposal to proofread it. Have at least 2-6 extra set of "eyes" look over the project.

- Get letters of recommendation/support.

- Form partnerships. Proposals have a better chance at getting funded if they show that you are working together with others.

- Last but never least; always thank those organizations and individuals that have supported your initiative.

"Most people do not recognize opportunity because it is disguised as hard work."

— **Benjamin Franklin**
Author, Politician, Scientist

Chapter 24
SALES

Selling Your Stuff

Successful Sales: Developing a Plan

Many entrepreneurs and business owners know that their business can be successful through sales, but many professionals don't have a plan for getting new business.

They might count on random acts of networking, lunches out, occasional lunch or dinner meetings, phone contacts, and some follow-up to stay in touch.

However, to be successful an actual plan of action needs to be created. A plan that is written out, reviewed and followed. If your plan isn't working then change it, but do have a plan. The following steps are activities that will help you start developing your sales plan.

Step 1: Who is your ideal client or customer?

This is a step that is so often missed. It is often one of the most challenging steps when building a sales plan. However, if you complete this step, then the rest is done with a lot less struggle.

You cannot be all things to all people or serve everyone. Once you pick an area to specialize, then work with that area. As you develop that area you will become an expert in your business. More success will come to you once you decide to focus on a specialization.

Who is your ideal client?

Is there a dollar amount of sales they have achieved – is there an age group of a company that you want to do business with?

- Is there a growth stage?

- Size? Industry? Geographic area?

- Number of employees? Family members important?

- Who is the person you need to deal with - CEO – Owner, - Dept head, etc

- Is it an individual? Age requirement or limit?

- Marital status? (for individual clients)

- Occupation? (for individual clients)

- Income? (for individuals)

- Location – where do they live? Is this important?

Once you have selected your ideal client or customer then figure out your principles. How are you going to serve your clients?

Step 2: What are your principle-based commitments to your clients?

You can choose important principles to guide your client's relationships. Principles that will help you make firm commitments to your clients.

This exercise will inspire your clients and referral partners that you begin to develop and will increase your enthusiasm for your work.

Make a list of your principles that you believe are important. These could be: customer service, confidentiality, security, competency, quality, on-time delivery, respect etc.

Then list the commitments or guidelines that you would be willing to make to your clients.

It is a good idea that not only you, as a business owner that is just starting out, but also your salespeople each fill out a plan of action. That way there is more accountability on behalf of the salesperson to achieve the principals he has set for himself to commit to.

Technology on your side

The right technology can significantly improve your selling efficiency. For best results, give your sales people the training and technical support they need to use it.

A. If you have many high-value customers and prospects, customer relationship management (CRM) software can be an invaluable tool.

- Get CRM software from a supplier with knowledge of your industry.

- Make sure the software lets you generate the reports you need. For example, you should be able to analyze and group your customers using different criteria.

- If necessary, make sure data can be transferred and stored across different sites.

- Feed in data from different parts of your business. For example, a sales rep should be able to see if customers are over their agreed credit limit before selling them new products.

B. Use appropriate technology to improve selling activities.

- For example, you might provide your field sales reps with remote access to your intranet, so they can check warehouse supplies and input orders while on the customer's premises.

TIP:

As with everything, practice makes perfect. You may want to lower your rates or volunteer your company for a few projects at the beginning of your company to become familiar with the "sales" process. Another idea is to "shadow" a sales rep (your insurance agent, pharmaceutical sales rep, your realtor, etc.) for a day to see how they prepare for a sales appointment. I highly recommend reading a book titled Selling to VITO (The Very Important Top Officer) by Anthony Parinello.

"For tomorrow belongs to the people who prepare for it today"

— African Proverb

Chapter 25
THE FUTURE OF THE LANGUAGE INDUSTRY
Where to Go From Here

Once things are going smoothly you can look into expansion and diversification of your services. You can get rid of things that you don't like and replace them with systems you develop on your own or from other language agencies you come into contact with. The language industry is an ever-changing industry, it is vital that you keep up with the changes and innovation to stay competitive.

There will be no end to your learning, especially in business. The more you learn, the more you protect your business interests and business endeavors. Over the years I have learned to do things that at the beginning I had to outsource until I had the time and patience to figure it out (web design, taxes, accounting, etc.). I now do several of these things myself, not just to save money, but to keep a close eye on my business and the way it is perceived in the public.

Complimentary Businesses

Below are examples of businesses that you could do in conjunction with your language interpreting and/or translation business:

- Full Service Advertising/Marketing Agency

- Ongoing training (development of training center)

- 24-hour answering/call service (Multilingual)

- Language Software reseller (ex. Rosetta Stone)

- Software and Equipment upgrades

- Language Instructor

- Language Tutor

- English Instructor

- ESL Instructor

- Immigration Services Consultant

- Bilingual Tax Preparer/Consultant

- Cultural Event Planner

- Bilingual Phone Interpreting

- Travel Agency (bilingual market focus)

- Executive Recruitment Firm (Bilingual/International focus)

As with most things it will take a little research and a lot of practice to get everything working the way you like it. From time to time you may need to revisit chapters in this book to remind yourself of issues and areas that were not of concern the first time you read the book. I encourage you to visit our companion website: www.desototranslations.com for more information.

Good Luck!

www.DESOTOTRANSLATIONS.com

Appendix

Interpreting/Translation Invoice & Estimate Samples

XYZ, Inc.
555 Anywhere St.
Los Angeles, CA 12345
Phone: (269) 555-5555
FAX: (269) 555-5100

Estimate

Name / Address	
ATTN: HealthNetwork	
Brian Adams	

Date: 3-Nov-09
Terms: Due Upon Completion

Description	Total
General Document Translation (English to Spanish translations)	
Temp Visitor Policy	$50.00
PROJECT TOTAL	**$50.00**

XYZ guarantees that all work will be completed to satisfaction and in a timely manner.

XYZ, Inc.
jane@xyz.com

XYZ Interpreting, Inc.
1234 Anywhere St.
Fun Time, CA. 46888
Phone: (555) 423-5678

INVOICE

Name / Address	
ATTN: Digital Advertising, Inc	
John	

Date: 11-May-10
Terms: Due Upon Receipt

Description	Total
ON-SITE INTERPRETING SERVICES	
Spanish to English	$100.00
2 hrs x $50 per hour	
PROJECT TOTAL	**$100.00**

XYZ guarantees all work will be completed to satisfaction and in a timely manner.

*XYZ will place a footnote at bottom of project with date of translation for
record keeping purposes and accountability of the translation

XYZ, Inc.
anyone@anywhere.com

Appendix B:

Ethics

Some of these ethics are from the National Association of Social Workers website (http://www. socialworkers.org/pubs/code/code.asp) and from the American Translators Association, different ethics apply to translators and contractors based on industry, state, company you are working for and the client you are working with:

Interpreter & Translator Ethics Overview
For translators, it is important to translate the text faithfully and in full to satisfy the needs of the end user(s). The main things to uphold are:

1. Mastery of the target language equivalent to that of an educated native speaker,

2. Up-to-date knowledge of the subject material and its terminology in both languages,

3. Access to information resources and reference materials, and knowledge of the tools of my profession,

4. Continuing efforts to improve, broaden, and deepen my skills and knowledge.

Also:
-Be truthful about qualifications and do not accept any assignments for which you are not fully qualified. Don't be afraid to admit that some things may be out of reach for you.

-Safeguard the interests of clients as your own and divulge no confidential information.

-Notify clients of any unresolved difficulties. If you cannot resolve a dispute, you should seek arbitration.

-Use a client as a reference only if you are prepared to name a person to attest to the quality of your work. In other words, double check you work.

-Respect and refrain from interfering with or supplanting any business relationship between your client and your client's client.

As employers or contractors of translators, you should uphold the above standards in business and further commit yourself to these practices:

-Put your contractual relationship with translators in writing and state expectations prior to work.

-Adhere to agreed terms, payment schedules, and agreed changes, and do not capriciously change job descriptions after work has begun.

-Deal directly with the translator about any dispute. If you cannot resolve a dispute, seek arbitration.

-Do not require translators to do unpaid work for the prospect of a paid assignment.

-Do not use translators' credentials in bidding or promoting your business without their consent or without the bona fide intention to use their services.

- For translations for publication or performance over which you have direct control, give translators recognition traditionally given authors.

Other common codes of ethics for companies include:
-Be professional at all times, first and foremost

-Translators shall keep all assignment-relation information strictly confidential

-Translators shall strive to further knowledge and skills through participation in workshops, professional meetings, interaction with professional colleagues, and reading of current literature in the field.

-Translators shall not approach any of the company's clients directly and attempt to sell their services. It is unethical and viewed as commercial piracy.

Confidentiality
Much of what you will be involved in is has been developed and paid for by one of your clients, or it may be potentially private agency business. This is privileged information that is confidential and you are expected to contribute to the work with confidentiality in mind. Do not discuss details of your client's work or the agency's business outside of work

Be sure to check into state laws involving other practices of ethics and regulatory rules for companies since they vary from state to state. It also may be a good idea to gain Human Resource advice as your company develops

1. Translators' Ethical Responsibilities to Clients

1.01 Physical Contact

Translators should not engage in physical contact with clients. Translators who engage in appropriate physical contact with clients are responsible for setting clear, appropriate, and culturally sensitive boundaries that govern such physical contact.

1.02 Sexual Harassment

Translators should not sexually harass clients. Sexual harassment includes sexual advances, sexual solicitation, requests for sexual favors, and other verbal or physical conduct of a sexual nature.

1.03 Derogatory Language

Translators should not use derogatory language in their written or verbal communications to or about clients. Translators should use accurate and respectful language in all communications to and about clients.

2. Translators' Ethical Responsibilities to Colleagues

2.01 Respect

(a) Translators should treat colleagues with respect and should represent accurately and fairly the qualifications, views, and obligations of colleagues.

(b) Translators should avoid unwarranted negative criticism of colleagues in communications with clients or with other professionals. Unwarranted negative criticism may include demeaning comments that refer to colleagues' level of competence or to individuals' attributes such as race, ethnicity, national origin, color, sex, sexual orientation, age, marital status, political belief, religion, and mental or physical disability.

(c) Translators should cooperate with colleagues and with colleagues of other professions when such cooperation serves the well-being of clients.

2.02 Confidentiality

Translators should respect confidential information shared by colleagues in the course of their professional relationships and transactions. Translators should ensure that such colleagues understand Translators' obligation to respect confidentiality and any exceptions related to it.

2.03 Disputes Involving Colleagues

(a) Translators should not take advantage of a dispute between a colleague and an employer to obtain a position or otherwise advance the Translators' own interests.

(b) Translators should not exploit clients in disputes with colleagues or engage clients in any inappropriate discussion of conflicts between translators and their colleagues.

2.04 Unethical Conduct of Colleagues
(a) Translators should take adequate measures to discourage, prevent, expose, and correct the unethical conduct of colleagues.

(b) Translators should be knowledgeable about established policies and procedures for handling concerns about colleagues' unethical behavior. Translators should be familiar with national, state, and local procedures for handling ethics complaints. These include policies and procedures created by ATA, licensing and regulatory bodies, employers, agencies, and other professional organizations.

(c) Translators who believe that a colleague has acted unethically should seek resolution by discussing their concerns with the colleague when feasible and when such discussion is likely to be productive.

(d) When necessary, translators who believe that a colleague has acted unethically should take action through appropriate formal channels (such as contacting a state licensing board or regulatory body, an ATA committee on inquiry, or other professional ethics committees).

(e) Translators should defend and assist colleagues who are unjustly charged with unethical conduct.

3. Translators' Ethical Responsibilities in Practice Settings

3.01 Education and Training
(a) Translators who function as educators, field instructors for students, or trainers should provide instruction only within their areas of knowledge and competence and should provide instruction based on the most current information and knowledge available in the profession.

(b) Translators who function as educators or field instructors for students should evaluate students' performance in a manner that is fair and respectful.

(c) Translators who function as educators or field instructors for students should take reasonable steps to ensure that clients are routinely informed when services are being provided by students.

(d) Translators who function as educators or field instructors for students should not engage in any dual or multiple relationships with students in which there is a risk of exploitation or potential harm to the student. Translator educators and field instructors are responsible for setting clear, appropriate, and culturally sensitive boundaries.

3.02 Continuing Education and Staff Development

Translators, administrators and supervisors should take reasonable steps to provide or arrange for continuing education and staff development for all staff for which they are responsible. Continuing education and staff development should address current knowledge and emerging developments related to social work practice and ethics.

4. Translators' Ethical Responsibilities as Professionals

4.01 Competence

(a) Translators should accept responsibility or employment only on the basis of existing competence or the intention to acquire the necessary competence.

(b) Translators should strive to become and remain proficient in professional practice and the performance of professional functions. Translators should critically examine and keep current with emerging knowledge relevant to translation. Translators should routinely review the professional literature and participate in continuing education relevant to translation practice and translation ethics.

(c) Translators should base practice on recognized knowledge, including empirically based knowledge, relevant to translation and translation ethics.

4.02 Discrimination

Translators should not practice, condone, facilitate, or collaborate with any form of discrimination on the basis of race, ethnicity, national origin, color, sex, sexual orientation, age, marital status, political belief, religion, or mental or physical disability.

4.03 Private Conduct

Translators should not permit their private conduct to interfere with their ability to fulfill their professional responsibilities.

4.04 Dishonesty, Fraud, and Deception

Translators should not participate in, condone, or be associated with dishonesty, fraud, or deception.

4.05 Impairment

(a) Translators should not allow their own personal problems, psychosocial distress, legal problems, substance abuse, or mental health difficulties to interfere with their professional judgment and performance or to jeopardize the best interests of people for whom they have a professional responsibility.

(b) Translators whose personal problems, psychosocial distress, legal problems, substance abuse, or mental health difficulties interfere with their professional judgment and performance should immediately seek consultation and take appropriate remedial action by seeking professional help, making adjustments in workload, terminating practice, or taking any other steps necessary to protect clients and others.

4.06 Misrepresentation
(a) Translators should make clear distinctions between statements made and actions engaged in as a private individual and as a representative of the social work profession, a professional translation organization, or the translator's employing agency.

(b) Translators who speak on behalf of professional social work organizations should accurately represent the official and authorized positions of the organizations.

(c) Translators should ensure that their representations to clients, agencies, and the public of professional qualifications, credentials, education, competence, affiliations, services provided, or results to be achieved are accurate. Translators should claim only those relevant professional credentials they actually possess and take steps to correct any inaccuracies or misrepresentations of their credentials by others.

4.07 Solicitations
(a) Translators should not engage in uninvited solicitation of potential clients who, because of their circumstances, are vulnerable to undue influence, manipulation, or coercion.

(b) Translators should not engage in solicitation of testimonial endorsements (including solicitation of consent to use a client's prior statement as a testimonial endorsement) from current clients or from other people who, because of their particular circumstances, are vulnerable to undue influence.

4.08 Acknowledging Credit
(a) Translators should take responsibility and credit, including authorship credit, only for work they have actually performed and to which they have contributed.

(b) Translators should honestly acknowledge the work of and the contributions made by others.

5. Translators' Ethical Responsibilities to the Translation Profession
5.01 Integrity of the Profession
(a) Translators should work toward the maintenance and promotion of high standards of practice.

(b) Translators should uphold and advance the values, ethics, knowledge, and mission of the profession. Translators should protect, enhance, and improve the integrity of the profession through appropriate study and research, active discussion, and responsible criticism of the profession.

(c) Translators should contribute time and professional expertise to activities that promote respect for the value, integrity, and competence of the translation profession. These activities may include teaching, research, consultation, service, legislative testimony, presentations in the community, and participation in their professional organizations.

(d) Translators should contribute to the knowledge base of translation and share with colleagues their knowledge related to practice, research, and ethics. Translators should seek to con-tribute to the profession's literature and to share their knowledge at professional meetings and conferences.

(e) Translators should act to prevent the unauthorized and unqualified practice of translations.

5.02 Evaluation and Research
(a) Translators should monitor and evaluate policies, the implementation of programs, and practice interventions.

(b) Translators should promote and facilitate evaluation and research to contribute to the development of knowledge.

(c) Translators should critically examine and keep current with emerging knowledge relevant to translation and fully use evaluation and research evidence in their professional practice.

(d) Translators engaged in evaluation or research should carefully consider possible consequences and should follow guidelines developed for the protection of evaluation and research participants. Appropriate institutional review boards should be consulted.

(e) Translators engaged in evaluation or research should obtain voluntary and written informed consent from participants, when appropriate, without any implied or actual deprivation or penalty for refusal to participate; without undue inducement to participate; and with due regard for participants' well-being, privacy, and dignity. Informed consent should include information about the nature, extent, and duration of the participation requested and disclosure of the risks and benefits of participation in the research.

(f) When evaluation or research participants are incapable of giving informed consent, translators should provide an appropriate explanation to the participants, obtain the participants' assent to the extent they are able, and obtain written consent from an appropriate proxy.

(g) Translators should never design or conduct evaluation or research that does not use consent procedures, such as certain forms of naturalistic observation and archival research, unless rigorous and responsible review of the research has found it to be justified because of its prospective scientific, educational, or applied value and unless equally effective alternative procedures that do not involve waiver of consent are not feasible.

(h) Translators should inform participants of their right to withdraw from evaluation and research at any time without penalty.

(i) Translators should take appropriate steps to ensure that participants in evaluation and research have access to appropriate supportive services.

(j) Translators engaged in evaluation or research should protect participants from unwarranted physical or mental distress, harm, danger, or deprivation.

(k) Translators engaged in the evaluation of services should discuss collected information only for professional purposes and only with people professionally concerned with this information.

(l) Translators engaged in evaluation or research should ensure the anonymity or confidentiality of participants and of the data obtained from them. Social workers should inform participants of any limits of confidentiality, the measures that will be taken to ensure confidentiality, and when any records containing research data will be destroyed.

(m) Translators who report evaluation and research results should protect participants' confidentiality by omitting identifying information unless proper consent has been obtained authorizing disclosure.

(n) Translators should report evaluation and research findings accurately. They should not fabricate or falsify results and should take steps to correct any errors later found in published data using standard publication methods.

(o) Translators engaged in evaluation or research should be alert to and avoid conflicts of interest and dual relationships with participants, should inform participants when a real or potential conflict of interest arises, and should take steps to resolve the issue in a manner that makes participants' interests primary.

(p) Translators should educate themselves, their students, and their colleagues about responsible research practices.

6. Translators' Ethical Responsibilities to the Broader Society

6.01 Public Emergencies

Translators should provide appropriate professional services in public emergencies to the greatest extent possible.

Glossary of Terms

Accounts Receivable
A record used to account for the total number of sales made through the extension of credit.

Accreditation
Currently, there is no licensing or certifying of translators in the United States; however, the American Translators Association offers an "accreditation program" by which they will test an individual in a given language combination route (for example, English to Spanish or Spanish to English) and provide them with accreditation upon passing the exam.

Accrual Basis
An accounting method used for recordkeeping purposes where all income and expenses are charged to the period to which they apply, regardless of whether money has been received.

Adaptation
1: something that is adapted; *specifically*: A composition rewritten into a new form.

2: localization procedure through which the translator replaces a culture-specific aspect of a product, service, or document, such as a software utility, color, icon, or other cultural artifact from the source culture with an equivalent appropriate to the target culture to accommodate the expectations of the target audience.

Balance Sheet
A financial statement used to report a business's total assets, liabilities and equity.

Bonding
Generally used by service companies as a guarantee to their clients that they have the necessary ability and financial backing to meet their obligations.

Business Plan
A plan used to chart a new or ongoing business's strategies, sales projections, and key personnel in order to obtain financing and provide a strategic foundation a business can use to grow.

Break-Even Analysis
An analysis method used to determine the number of jobs or products that need to be sold to reach a break-even point in a business.

Capitalization
Every company has capital-either in the form of money, common stock, long-term debt, or in some combination of all three. It is possible to have too much capital, in which case the firm is overcapitalized or too little capital, in which case the firm is undercapitalized.

Cash Basis
An accounting method used for recordkeeping where income is logged when received and expenses charged when they occur.

Certified
Having or proved by a certificate.

Certified Interpreter
A person who provides an oral translation between speakers who speak different languages, who also has a certificate in interpreting from a university or certification testing and assessing organization.

Certified Translation
The rendering of something into another language or into one's own from another language that is conducted or proofread by someone that is certified.

Certified Translator/Interpreter
The interpreter/translator certification identifies individuals that have taken and passed testing and or training that has documented their abilities, credentials and education. This certification is commonly requested in courts, hospitals, and other agencies using interpreters and translators to validate their skills and training. This also allows you to certify documents translated by the interpreter/translator.

Collateral
Assets used as security for the extension of a loan.

Commercial Loans
A short-term loan usually issued for a term of six months.

Computer-Assisted Translation (CAT)
Translation in which a variety of computer programs (tools) are used to support the task of human translation.

Conditional Sales Contract
A credit contract used for the purchase of equipment where the purchase of equipment where the purchaser doesn't receive title of the equipment until the amount specified in the contract has been paid in full.

Contraction
1. A shortening of a word, syllable, or word group by omission of a sound or letter; *also*: a form produced by such shortening.

2. Natural decrease in the amount of text used in the target language to express the same semantic content (meaning) as compared to the corresponding segment in the source text.

Controlled Language
Subset of a language with restricted grammar, domain-specific vocabulary, and constrained style designed to allow domain specialists to formulate unambiguous texts pertaining to their subject field.

Demographic Characteristics
The attributes such as income, age, and occupation that best describe your target market.

Depreciation
The depreciation in value of fixed assets that provides the foundation for a tax deduction based on either the declining-balance or straight-line method.

Disclosure Document Program
A form of protection that safeguards an idea while it is in its developmental stage.

Dun & Bradstreet
An agency which furnishes subscribers with market statistics and the financial standings and credit ratings of businesses.

Editor
1. Someone who edits especially as an occupation.

2. Bilingual member of the translation team who compares a completed translation to the source text for the purpose of validation the accuracy of the final target text, and gives the detailed feedback.

End User
Person who ultimately avails himself or herself of the translation, as opposed to various intermediate translation service providers who pass it on to the next client in a chain of suppliers.

Equipment Loans
 A loan used for the purchase of capital equipment.

Equity Capital
A form of financing where equity in a business is sold to private investors.

Estimate
An approximate judgment of calculation as of the value, amount, time size, or weight of something.

Expansion
1. Something that results from an act of expanding.

2. Natural increase in the amount of text used in the target language to Express the same semantic content (meaning) as compared to the corresponding segment in the source text.

Exploratory Research
A method used when gathering primary information for a market survey where targeted consumers are asked very general questions geared toward eliciting a lengthy answer.

Fictitious Name
Often referred to as a DBA, "Doing Business As," a fictitious name is frequently used by sole proprietors or partnerships to provide a name, other than those of the owners or partners, under which the business will operate.

Fixed Expenses
Expenses that must be paid each month and do not fluctuate with the slaves volume.

Flat Lease
A lease where the cost is fixed for a specific period of time.

Frequency
The number of times you hope to reach your target audience thorough your advertising campaign.

Gisting
Translation of a text for the purpose of providing the user with a general idea of the sense of the original, but without emphases on details or stylistic elegance.

Globalization
1. The act of process of globalizing: the state of being globalized; *especially* : the development of an increasingly integrated global economy market especially by free trade, free flow of capital, and the tapping of cheaper foreign labor markets.

Globalization (continued)
2. The business processes and allocation of resources necessary for taking a product to various markets around the globe.

GILT/G.I.L.T Industry
Globalization, Internationalization, Localization, and Translation (G.I.L.T), is an acronym given to any person or company that is involved in any of the aforementioned industries. Language interpreting is considered part of the GILT industry as well.

Glossary
1. A collection of textual glosses or of specialized terms with their meanings.

2. Terminological list of designations from a subject field, frequently with equivalents in one of more languages.

Idiom
A phrase of expression on which is understood in its common language and usage, but does not have a literal translation.

Income Statement
Also called an operating statement, an income statement charts the sales and operating costs of a business over a specific period of time, usually a month.

Interpretation
As a compared with translation, interpretation is the act of translating one language into another orally; relaying conversation between two individuals speaking different languages.

Interpreter
A person who provides an oral translation between speakers who speak different languages.

Internationalization
1. To make international.

2. Process of generalizing a product so that it can handle multiple languages, and cultural conventions (such as non-Roman scripts, varying date/time/currency formats, and so forth) without the need for substantial modification.

Investment Tax Credit
A tax credit that allows businesses to write off the first $10,000 of equipment purchased for business use.

Leasehold Improvements
The repairs and improvements made to a facility before occupation by the lessee.

Leveraging
1. To provide (as a corporation) or supplement (as money) with leverage; *also*: to enhance as if by supplying with financial leverage.

2. Reuse of resources (for example, terminology, segment of translated text, or formatting templates) from previously translated text.

Liability
A term used when analyzing insurance risks that describes possible areas of exposure. While there are numerous comprehensive and special coverage's that blanket almost every known exposure a business may be liable for, there are three forms of liability coverage that insurers usually will underwrite. The first is *general liability*, which covers any kind of bodily injury to nonemployees except that caused by automobiles and professional malpractice. The second is product liability, which covers injury to customers arising as a direct result of goods purchased from a business. The third is *public liability*, which covers injury to the public when they are on your premises.

Linguist
1. A person accomplished in languages; *especially*: one who speaks several languages.

2. A student or practitioner of linguistics, that is, of the science of language; a person proficient in more than one language.

Locale
1. A place or locality especially when viewed in relation to a particular event or characteristic.

2. In common practice, the language and the geographic region (for example, Spanish in Colombia versus Spanish in Spain) of a given target audience for a translation.

Localization

Cross-culture communications process of preparing locale-specific versions of a product or service, consisting of translation of textual material into the language and textual conventions of the target locale, and adaptation of non-textual materials as well as input, output, and delivery mechanisms to meet the cultural, technical, and regulatory requirements of the locale.

Machine Translation (MT)

Mode of translation in which a computer program analyzes a source text and produces a target text, typically without human intervention at the actual time of translation.

Market Survey

A research method used to define the market parameters of a business.

Markup

1. An amount added to the cost price to determine the selling price; broadly: profit.

2. Any text, tag, or code that is added to the data of a document to convey information about it.

Media Plan

A plan that details the usage of media in an advertising campaign including costs, running dates, markets, reach frequency, rationales, and strategies.

Metric

Procedure providing a means of measuring the quality of a product or service that results in a composite numeric value.

Net Profit on Sales

A profitability measure that determines the difference between net profit and operating costs.

Occupational Safety and Health Act (OSHA)

A federal law that requires employers to provide employees with a workplace that is free of hazardous conditions.

Overhead

Refers to all non-labor expenses needed to operate a business.

Partnership

A partnership is a legal for of business operation between two or more individuals. There are several types of partnerships that the federal government recognizes. The two most common are general and limited partnerships.

Personal Loans

Short-term loans that are extended based on the personal integrity of the borrower.

Point-of-Sale (POS) Systems

A computerized network that is operated by a miniframe computer and hooked to several check out terminals.

Post-editor

Translator who reviews a completed translation to validate the accuracy of the final target text with reference to the source text in order to ensure a defined degree of stylistic acceptability, and makes changes where necessary.

Post-project review

Review and performance evaluation procedure conducted at the end of a project to determine how well the project conformed to the original specifications.

Profit

There are generally two kinds of profits: gross profit and net profit. Gross profit is the difference between gross sales and cost of sales, while net profit is the difference between gross profit and all costs associated with operating a business.

Project Manager

Person who coordinates the various aspects of the project and ensures their proper execution.

Proof Reader

Reader of printed or electronic target text whose task is to find typographical and formatting errors and verify whether the text is understandable and reads well in the target language without reference to the source text.

Quote <estimate>

To state the current price of a product or service.

Reach

The total number of people within your target market that you reach through your advertising campaign.

Regionalism
In language, having characteristics specific to a certain geographic region.

Register
Set of properties associated with speech or writing that is characteristic of a particular type of linguistic text or speech and takes into account the nature of relationships among speakers, the subjects treated, and the degree of formality of familiarity of the text.

Requester
Individual, department, company, or organization placing an order for a translation.

Return On Investment (ROI)
A profit ability measure that evaluates the performance of a business by dividing net profit by total assets.

Romance Languages
Languages derived from "Vulgar Latin" (the every-day speech of the common people), such as Italian, Spanish, Portuguese, French, Romanian, etc.

Sight Translation
Oral translation, often impromptu, of a written text from one language to another in the presence of the end user with little or no prior examination on the part of the translator.

Simultaneous Interpretation
Someone who interprets for someone in another language while the speaker speaks without interruption. This is the opposite of consecutive interpreting, because a consecutive interpreter awaits his turn and does not start speaking until the speaker allows him the time to do so. Simultaneous interpreting is one of the most common kinds of interpreting, but also the most difficult. Very few translators (who are used to getting the time to really think about their translations) can do it, and not even all interpreters can do it well.

Sole Proprietor
A legal form of operation where only one owner can exist.

Source Language (SL)
Language from which a translation is produced.

Source Text
The text to be translated.

Subchapter S:
The Federal law which allows small corporations to pay out all income proportionately to its shareholders, who then claim the income on their personal income taxes.

Subject Matter Expert
Person with expertise in a subject area.

Sublet
This term refers to the lease of space within a rented facility by the original lessee.

Specific Research
A method used when gathering primary information for a market survey where targeted consumers are asked very specific and in-depth questions geared toward resolving problems found through exploratory research.

Target language (TL)
Language in which the translation is written.

Target Text (TT)
Text produced as the result of the translation process.

Term Extraction
Identification and compilation of translation relevant single or multiword terms from monolingual or aligned bilingual texts.

Terminology
Set of designations belonging to the language of a given subject field.

Terminology Database
Database containing data related to concepts or their designations or both.

Text Type
Class to which a text is assigned based on its function, format, or the specific intention of the author with respect to the target audience.

Third-Party Reviewer
Person assigned by the requester or suppler to evaluate a completed translation for quality or end-user suitability.

Translation <product>
Result of the translation process.

Translation <process>
Process comprising the creation of a written target text based on a source text in such a way that the content and in many cases, the form of the two texts, can be considered to be equivalent.

Translation Competence
Ability to translate the source text into the target language completely and accurately by choosing an equivalent expression in the target language that both fully conveys and best matches the meaning intended in the source language for the intended audience and purpose.

Translation Memory (TM)
Text-based resource consisting of aligned text segments (translation units) stored by a translation memory tool.

Translation Memory Tool
Computer program that facilitates comparison of new source text segments to previously translated source text in order to link them to existing translations.

Translation Quality
Degree to which the characteristics of a translation fulfill the requirements of the agreed upon specifications.

Translation ServiceProvider
Company, department, or individual approached by the requester, providing professional translation services into one or multiple languages for the requester.

Translation Team
Group of specialists assembled for the purposes of managing and producing a translation project, made up of, for example, a project manager, translator(s), editor(s), and possible a terminologist, desktop publisher, graphic artist, software engineer(s), post-editor(s), and so forth.

Translator
Communication specialist who produces the target text.

Variable Expenses
Business costs that fluctuate from each payment period according to the sales volume.

Venture Capital
A source of financing for either start-up or expansion capital that is based on providing private investors with equity positions within the business.

Word count
Number of words in a text that is, in the body, header, footer, text boxes, and so forth; more generally, the number of words in the content to be translated.

Worker's Compensation
A state or privately managed insurance fund that reimburses employees for injuries suffered on the job.

Working Capital
Net current assets required for the company to carry on with its work. It's the surplus of a firm's current assets over its current liabilities.

Appendix D:

Books, Websites and other Resources

Spanish-English general dictionaries:

- <u>Full-sized</u>: Oxford *Spanish-English dictionary* (3rd Ed. ISBN 0198604750) (there is also an abbreviated, cheap, but quite adequate version that works as a pop-up on your computer- search eBay; or a full sized with CD-ROM that is ISBN 0198608780).
- <u>Full-sized</u>: *Webster's New World International Spanish Dictionary (formerly Simon & Schuster's)*, ISBN 0764576437
- <u>Pocket-sized</u>: *Merriam-Webster's Spanish-English dictionary*, ISBN 087779-916-4, about $6.50 but full of Latin American terms. You can pick this up at your local bookstore.

Spanish-English legal dictionaries:

- *The Interpreter's Companion*, by Acebo **(www.acebo.com)** –available in pocket sized book and/or CD-ROM. Sections on everyday legal terms, medical (with anatomical diagrams), traffic (with diagrams), weapons (diagrams), slang, insults, sex
- *Diccionario de Términos Jurídicos ingles-español/ Spanish-English*, by Enrique Alcaraz Varo and Brian Hughes. (latest edition: ISBN 9788434432635). Extremely comprehensive.
- *Bilingual Law Dictionary/Diccionario Jurídico Bilingüe*, by Cuauhtémoc Gallegos, Merl Publications, ISBN 1886347034. Not a big book but great for neologisms.
- *Diccionario de terminología jurídica Mexicana*, Javier F. Becerra, ISBN 96862360802. Only Spanish> English but its greatest usefulness is for Mexican legal documents and speech.
- *Criminal Court Dictionary English-Spanish, Español-Inglés*, by Dennis McKenna, ISBN 0-9760801-1-7. Very specific to US courts, emphasis on Mexican Spanish.

Medical dictionary:

The Acebo will be enough for much of your court work, but if you want to have more depth and a searchable CD-ROM to go with it, try:

- Spanish-English English-Spanish Medical Dictionary, by Onyria Herrera McElroy and Lola L. Grabb, ISBN 0-7817-5011-3 – the CD-ROM install easily onto your hard disk for permanent reference. Has lots of phrases for different medical situations, and color diagrams.

Dictionary of idioms:

- *NTC's Dictionary of Phrasal Verbs and Other Idiomatic Verbal Phrases* by R. Spears, ISBN 0-8442-5462-2 (English)
- *Cassell's Colloquial Spanish: A Handbook of Idiomatic Usage*, by Arthur Bryson Gerrard, ISBN 0020794304 (Spanish)

False cognates:

- *Hamel's Comprehensive Bilingual Dictionary of Spanish False Cognates/Gran Diccionario de Falsos Amigos del Ingles*, ISBN 1-886835-07-1. Shows the common false uses as well as the correct ones- for both languages.

Grammar and usage:

- *A New Reference Grammar of Modern Spanish*, by John Butt & Carmen Benjamin, ISBN 007-144049-6. Nothing is more thorough.
- *Diccionario del uso del español*, by Maria Moliner. The definitive usage dictionary for Spanish. An abbreviated and therefore more affordable version is at ISBN 8424922646.
- *The Grammar Book: An ESL/EFL Teacher's Course*, by Celce-Murcia and Larsen-Freeman. ISBN 0838447252 (for English). Huge.

Slang:

Again, the Acebo book should help, and also see the list of books on regionalism. In addition:

- *Streetwise Spanish Dictionary/Thesaurus*, by Mary McVey Gill and Brenda Wegmann, ISBN 0844225517. Organized by topic, with notes on national origin.
- *Dictionary of Mexicanismos*, by D. McKenna, ISBN 0976080109.
- *Dictionary of American Slang* by R.L. Chapman. The definitive one that I grew up with and peeked into surreptitiously whenever I was alone at home! ISBN 006270107X, but there are also more abbreviated English slang dictionaries at Intransbooks.

Terminology Research Websites

General Terminology:
http://www.answers.com This is a good explanation tool, and often includes translations of a term into non-English languages. You can install a hot-key onto your computer so you can click on a term in any application and the answer page opens on your browser.

http://www.wikipedia.org User-developed encyclopedia in many languages- you can't always trust what you find!

http://www.wordreference.com translations into French & Spanish, as well as English-only dictionary.

http://www.rae.es – Diccionario de la Real Academia Española as well as an online Diccionario Panhispanico de Dudas. Both are fundamental.

http://www.acronymfinder.com – does what it says.

http://www.jergasdehablahispana.org – Slang from various countries.

http://www.proz.com/kudoz - A good online community of professional translators, with lots of terms you can look up and online glossaries. Explore this site!

http://www.onelook.com – Find more dictionaries online.

http://www-derecho.unex.es/biblioteca/diccionario.htm Diccionarios y Enciclopedias del Mundo.

http://www.glosarium.com La Web de los Glosarios Gratis

http://unterm.un.org/ - United Nations Multilingual Terminology Database- to see how UN agencies translate terms.

Idioms and Sayings

http://www.idiomsite.com – English

http://www.google.com/Top/World/Espa%C3%B1o1/Referencia/Refranes_y_dichos/
Spanish

Legal Resources

http://www.unitfr.ch/derechopenal/ley.htm Criminal codes from around the world in Spanish

http://www.glossarist.com/glossaries/law-justice Online law dictionaries

http://www.lexjuris.com – Puerto Rico law

http://www.mexicolegal.com.mx/m_help.htm Mexican legal resource.

http://mexicolaw.com/Table_of_Content.htm Mexican law in English

http://sdnyinterpreters.org/pub/term by and for court interpreters- NY

http://utcourts.gov/resources/interp/glossary.asp Utha courts

http://www.courtinfo.ca.gov/selfhelp/espanol/glosario.htm California courts

http://www.proz.com/glossary-translations/english-to-spanish-translations/77
Working translatiors' English-Spanish legal glossaries

http://www.proz.com/glossary-translations/spanish-to-english-translations/77
working translators' Spanish-English legal glossaries.

Online Legal Interpreting/Translating Resources

http://www.najit.org join the NAJIT listserv- lots of Spanish-language vocabulary discussions straight from court interpreting situations- for NAJIT members only

http://groups.google.com/group/interpreterandtranslator?hl=en Judicial Interpreters and Translators Group- open to all who sign up, aimed at US court interpreters

http://finance.groups.yahoo.com/group/legaltranslators join to get emails with legal translating questions & answers

http://groups.yahoo.com/group/GlossPost/?yguid=216880860 search for online glossaries

http://www.english-spanish-translator.org/enlgish-spanish-legal-translation

http://www.english-spanish-translator.org/spanish-english-legal-translation

Recommended References for Spanish Interpreters & Translators

Spanish-English Dictionaries

Oxford Spanish-English Dictionary (available on CD-ROM)

American Heritage Larousse Spanish-English Dictionary

Simon & Schuster's International Dcitionary

Larousse Spanish-English Dictionary

General Language References

Diccionario de ideas afines, by Fernando Corripio, pub. Editorial Herder

Diccionario de dudas y dificultades de la lengua española, by Manuel Seco, pub. Espasa Calpe

Diccionario del uso del español, by Maria Moliner, pub. Editorial Gredos Using Spanish Synonyms, by R.E. Bachelor, pub. Cambridge University Press.

Diccionario razonado de sinonimos y contrarios, by Jose M. Zainqui, pub.Editorial de Vecchi

NTC Dictionary of Spanish False Cognates, pub. National Textbook Company

A New Reference Grammar of Modern Spanish, by Butt & Benjamin, pub.McGraw-Hill

*American Heritage Dictionary of the English Language 3rd ed. American Heritage Publishing Co., Inc. and Houghton Mifflin Co. 1996.
ISBN 0-395-44895-6. Benson, M., Benson, E. and Illson, R. (Ed.). The BBI Combinatory*

Dictionary of English: A Guide to Word Combinations John Benjamins, 1986 ASIN: 0-915-02780-1.

Colce-Murcia, M. and Larsen-Freeman, D. The Grammar Book: An ESL/EFL Teacher's Course. Heinle & Heilen, 1998. ISBN: 0-838-44725-2

Greenbaum, S. and Quirk, R. A Student's Grammar of the English Language.Addison-Wesley, 1990. ISBN 0-582-05971-2.

Spears, R. NTC's Dictionary of Phrasal Verbs and Other Idiomatic Verbal Phrases National Testbook Company, 1993. ISBN 0-8442-5462-2.

Legal Dictionaries

Bilingual Law Dictionary/Diccionario Juridico Bilingüe, by Cuauhtémoc Gallegos, Merl Publications

Bilingual Dictionary of Criminal Justice Terms, By Benmaman, Connolly & Loos, pub. Gould

Diccionario de términos jurídicos, by Hughes and Alcaraz Varo, pub. Ariel

Diccionario de terminología jurídica mexicana, by Javier F. Becerra, pub.Escuela Libre de Derecho

Regional Spanish

Argentina

Dis, Emilio. Código Lunfardo. Editorial Caburé, 1975.

Escobar, Raúl Tomas. Diccionario del hampa y del delito: lunfardo latinoamericano, drogadicción, "punk", insurrección, mitología, voces vulgares y populares. Ediciones Universidad, 1986.

Gabello, José. Nuevo diccionario lunfardo. Ediciones Corregidor, 1994. ISBN 950-05-0565-8

Chile

Subercaseaux, Miguel. Diccionario de chilenismos. Editorial Juvenil, 1986.

Costa Rica

Pacheco, Miguel Q. Nuevo diccionario de costarriqueñismos. Publisher unknown. ISBN 9977660557

Cuba

Sánchez –Boudy, José. Diccionario de Cubanismos más usuales (Como habla el cubano). Ediciones Universal, 1978. ISBN 0-89729-199-9

El Salvador

Geoffroy Rivas, Pedro. El español que hablamos en El Salvador. Ministerio de Educación, Dirección de Publicaciones, San Salvador, El Salvador, 1982.

Latin America

Lipski, John M. Latin American Spanish. Longman, 1994. ISBN 0-58208-760-0

México

Cabrera, Luis. Diccionario de Aztequismos. Editorial Oasis, 1975.

Galvan, Roberto A. and Teschner, Richard V. El diccionario del español chicano.National Textbook Company, 1985 ISBN 0-8325-9634-5

Gomez de Silva, Guido. Diccionario Breve de Mexicanismos. Academia Mexicana, Fondo de Cultura Economica, 2001. ISBN 968-16-6408-6

Hamel, Bernard H. Hamel's Bilingual Dictionary of Mexican Spanish. Bilingual Book Press, 1994. ISBN 1-886835-01-4

Mejia Prieto, Jorge. Así habla el mexicano: Diccionario básico de mexicanismo. Panorama Editorial, S.A., 1984. ISBN 968-38-0122-6

Robinson, Linton H. Mexican Slang: A ¡*#@%&+! Guide. Bueno Books, 1992. ISBN 0-9627080-7-0

Perú

Bendezu Neyra, Guillermo E. Argot Limeño o Jerga Criolla del Perú. Editorial Lima, S.A., no date.

De Arona, Juan. Diccionario de peruanismos. Biblioteca Peruana, 1975.

Puerto Rico

Altieri de Barreto, Carmen G. El Lexico de la Delincuencia en Puerto Rico. Editorial Universitaria, Universidad de Puerto Rico, 1973.

Gallo, Cristino. Language of the Puerto Rico Street: A Slang Dictionary with English Cross-Reference. Book service of Puerto Rico, 1980.

Llorens, Washington. El habla popular de Puerto Rico. Editorial Edil, 1974.

Spain

Leon, Victor. Diccionario de argot español. Alianza Editorial, 1988. ISBN 84-206-1766-0

Slang and Colloquial Usage

Berger, Frances de Talavera. ¡Mierda! The Real Spanish You Were Never Taught in School. Plume, 1990. ISBN 0-452-26424-3

Burke, David. Street Spanish: How to Speak and Understand Spanish Slang. John Wiley & Sons, Inc., 1991. ISBN 0-471-52846-3

Burke, David. Street Spanish Slang Dictionary & Thesaurus. John Wiley & Sons, Inc., 1999. ISBN 0-471-16834-3

Cruz, Bill and Teck, Bill. The Official Spanglish Dictionary. Fireside-Simon & Schuster, 1998. ISBN 0-684-85412-0

Pierson, Raymond H. Guide to Spanish Idioms. Passport Books, 1992. ISBN 0-8442-7325-2

Polkinhorn, Harry; Velasco, Alfredo; and Lambert, Malcom. El libro de caló. Floricante Press, 1988.

Rosensweig, Jay B. Calo: Gutter Spanish. E.P. Dutton & Co., Inc. 1973. ISBN 0-525-47346-7

Where to Buy Dictionaries
In Trans Book Service
P.O. Box 467
Kinderhook, NY 12106-Fax: 518 758 6702
www.intransbooks.com

Useful Websites

http://www.englishclub.com/ (English grammar questions)

http://www3.unileon.es/dp/dfh/jmr/dicci/007.htm (Diccionarios de variantes del español)

http://buscon.rae.es/diccionario/drae.htm (Diccionario de la Lengua Española Real Academia)

http://europa.eu.int/eurodicautom/Contoller (Eurodicautom)

http://www.elcastellano.org/ (La Pagina del Idioma Español)

http://www.jerfasdehablahispana.org/ (Jergas de habla hispana)

http://sdnyinterpreters.org/term/ (Court Interpreters Office, Southern District of New York, Spanish-English glossary)

Resources to Develop Interpreting Skills

Many of the institutions listed below offer "academic certificates," which are different from state or federal interpreter certifications. If you receive academic certificates, and are not state or federally certified, you should clearly identify the certificate in your resumes or biographies and not claim state or federal interpreter certification. To do so would be unethical.

Colleges and Universities

BINGHAMTON UNIVERSITY
Translation Research & Instruction Program
Library Tower 1302
P.O. Box 6000
Binghamton, NY 13902
(607) 777-6726
http://www.binghamton.edu/trip
trip@binghamton.edu
The Translation Research and Instruction Program is the pedagogical division of the Center for Research in Translation (CRIT). It administers the interdisciplinary curriculum and examination that lead to translator certification. Although most students in the program are matriculated in one of the University degree programs, the translation study courses may be taken as a separate track.

BOSTON UNIVERSITY
Interpreter Certificate Program (Portuguese)
Center for Professional Education
940 Commonwealth Avenue West
Boston, MA 02215
(617) 353-4497
http://www.butrain.com/cpe/legalcert.asp
CPE@BU.EDU

BROOKDALE COMMUNITY COLLEGE
Community Interpreting in Spanish Certificate Program
Business and Community Development
765 Newman Springs Road
Lincoln, NJ 07738-1543
(732) 224-2315
www.brookdalecc.edu
The community need for interpreting Spanish to English is critical. The ability to overcome language barriers is essential in a variety of instances that include medical emergencies as well as legal and social situations. This program is designated to train entry-level interpreters for service and employment opportunities. The instructors-all

specialists in their respective fields of interpreting-will incorporate "real life" samples of materials and examples of situations that will be encountered in the field. Consecutive interpreting used in medical, legal, and social service situations, as well as simultaneous and sight translation will be covered. Advanced training for the state exam for Court Interpreters will be offered.

COLLEGE OF CHARLESTON

Dr. Virginia Benmaman, Director
MA Program in Bilingual Legal Interpreting
University of Charleston
Charleston, SC 29424-0001
(843) 953-4947
http://www.cofc.edu/~legalint

Masters Degree Program Description The Masters of Arts in Bilingual Legal Interpreting for English-Spanish is the only graduate program in the United States which offers the opportunity to receive the education and training required and expected of a professional degree-holding legal interpreter. The program is a comprehensive, sequenced, and integrated series of courses designed to provide the student with the theoretical foundation, performance competencies, and research skills required of a graduate entering this growing profession. The curriculum consists of 14 courses (42 credits) which can be completed over a two-year period. Eight of the ten courses must be completed at the University of Charleston during two full summers. The teaching faculty who are invited to teach during the summer sessions are among the most qualified professors of interpreting and professional interpreters in North America. The remaining two core courses, a practicum in legal settings and an internship as an apprentice interpreter, may be completed in a court jurisdiction of the student's choice. Four remaining courses may be taken at another university, subject to approval by the program director, and applied to the program as transfer credit.

Certificate Program Description This certificate program, comprised of existing courses within the present master's program, will provide the means by which students enrolled in the other language oriented graduate programs, as well as other interpreting and translating professionals, can attain the foundational skills in legal interpreting in an abbreviated time frame, generally
in one full summer. Students in the program will take four of the courses regularly offered during the summer session.

KEAN UNIVERSITY
Department of Foreign Languages, Literatures, and Cultures
Hutchinson Hall, J-309
Union, New Jersey 07083-0411
http://www.kean.edu/

MARYMOUNT MANHATTAN COLLEGE

221 East 71st Street
New York, NY 10021
(212) 774-0780
http://marymount.mmm.edu/

MONTCLAIR STATE UNIVERSITY

Certificate Program in Translation and Interpretation in Spanish
Maria Jose Vizcaino, Director
Spanish/Italian Department
Montclair State University
Upper Montclair, NJ 07043
(973) 655-4285
http://chss2.montclair.edu/spanish-italian/stranslation.htm
Montclair State University's Certificate Program in Translation and Interpretation in
Spanish provides basic preparation for entry-level translating and interpreting positions
in government, telecommunications, the judiciary, the helping professions, business and
the arts. Designed for students who have good speaking and writing skills in both English
and Spanish, the four-course sequence focuses on the specific skills of translation and
interpretation.

MONTCLAIR STATE UNIVERSITY

Department of French, German, and Russian
Montclair State University
Upper Montclair, NJ 07043
(973) 655-7422
http://chss2.montclair.edu/french
This department offers a Translation Concentration for French Majors.

NEW YORK UNIVERSITY

SCHOOL OF CONTINUING AND PROFESSIONAL STUDIES
Center for Foreign Languages and Translation
NYU School of Continuing and Professional Studies
10 Astor Place, Suite 505
New York, NY 10003
(212) 998-7030
http://www.scps.nyu.edu
scps.foreignlanguages@nyu.edu
Certificate in Court Interpreting
        Spanish/English
http://www.scps.nyu.edu/departments/certificate.jsp?cerld'155
This program is designed for individuals with mastery of both languages. As a
prerequisite to entering the program, all prospective students must pass an oral

proficiency test both in Spanish and English to determine their linguistic competence and general cultural preparation.
Certificate in Translation
        English to Spanish or Spanish to English
http://scps.nyu.edu/departments/certificate.jsp?cerld'157
This program is intended for linguistically skilled individuals of diverse professional and educational backgrounds who seek to develop abilities in the field of translation.
Certificate in Translation
        French to English, German to English, English to Portuguese, General Translation
http://www.scps.nyu.edu/dycon/acfl/cert tran.html
This program is intended for linguistically skilled individuals of diverse professional and educational backgrounds who seek to develop abilities in the field of translation.
Online Certificate Programs
http://scps.nyu.edu/departments/certificate.jsp?cerld'157
This program is available to distance learning students.

RIDER UNIVERSITY
Department of Foreign Languages and Literatures
Rider University
2083 Lawrenceville Road
Lawrenceville, NJ 08648
609-896-5146
forlang@Rider.edu
http://www.rider.edu/

RUTGERS UNIVERSITY
Department of Spanish & Portuguese
Faculty of Arts & Sciences
Rutgers, The State University
P.O. Box 270
New Brunswick, NJ 08903-0270
(732) 932-9412 x. 25
http://span-port.Rutgers.edu/
span-port@rci.rutgers.edu/
or http://french.rutgers.edu
Certificate of Proficiency in Spanish-English and English-Spanish Translation
OBJECTIVE: To provide students with the opportunity to gain competence in Spanish-English and English-Spanish translation. The program will train students in a skill which can be applied to future employment in connection with such major fields as Banking, Business, Journalism, Legal Translation and Social Services.

TEMPLE UNIVERSITY
Department of Spanish and Portuguese
Anderson Hall, Room 450
Philadelphia, PA 19122
(215) 204-1706
http://www.temple.edu/spanpor
haldaron@unix.temple.edu

UNION COUNTY COLLEGE
Interpreting Spoken Language Certificate Program
Elizabeth Campus E-500
12 West Jersey Street
Elizabeth, NJ 07201
(908) 965-2345
http://faculty.ucc.edu/fineart-difiore
The Interpreting Spoken Language Program trains bilingual individuals in the basic skills needed for professional work in interpreting and translating. Union County College offers three courses as part of a certificate program. Students from all language backgrounds may study in the program.

LANGUAGE REQUIREMENTS: A high level of proficiency in English and at least one other language is required for entrance into these courses. The College provides a placement test in English. Those wishing to study in this course must finish all developmental English and ESL requirements before registering for interpreting courses. Evaluation in one's other language is done by the student her/himself or in consultation with the coordinator of the program. It is recommended that the student have some college education in that language and be fluent both in speaking and writing.

UNIVERSITY OF ARIZONA
THE NATIONAL CENTER FOR INTERPRETATION
University of Arizona
Modern Languages Bldg., Room 445
Tucson, AZ 95721
(520) 621-3615
http://nci.arizona.edu/
ncitrp@u.arizona.edu
Summer Institute:
This is an intensive three-week course offered every summer to help beginning and intermediate court interpreters develop their interpretation abilities and to help advanced or working interpreters hone their skills. Advanced, intensive program alternatives are available for experienced federal and state certified interpreters.

Special Weekend Seminars (Friday-Sunday)

These will be held at least four times throughout the year in Tucson to assist candidates in preparing for the federal written and oral, as well as state, exams. In addition, traveling seminars are available to groups of 15 or more elsewhere.

UNIVERSITY OF MASSACHUSETTS-BOSTON

Division of Corporate, Continuing and Distance Education
University of Massachusetts, Boston
100 Morrissey Boulevard
Boston, MA 02125-3393
http://www.conted.umb.edu

DEPARTMENT OF HISPANIC STUDIES (617) 287-7550

This intensive six-credit undergraduate certificate program has been specially designed to provide qualified applicants with a comprehensive introduction to professional court interpretation. The program teaches the fundamentals of theory and practice through classroom discussion and activities, as well as through laboratory exercises designed to develop interpreting proficiency. Novice and experienced interpreters will benefit equally from extensive practice. Students will devote additional time out of class to court visits and to fulfill oral and written assignments. Not offered as an online course as of 2006.

WILLIAM PATTERSON UNIVERSITY

Center for continuing Education and Distance Learning
P.O. Box 913
Wayne, NJ 07474-0913
(973) 720-2491
http://www.wpunj.edu/ce

English Slang & Idioms References

DICTIONARY OF REGIONAL AMERICAN ENGLISH VOLS. I-IV.

Harvard University Press

DICTIONARY OF AMERICAN SLANG.

Harper Resource, 1998. ISBN 006270107X

THE BIG BOOK OF FILTH: 650 SEX SLANG WORDS AND PHRASES.

Sterling Publishing, 2000. ISBN 0304353507

ENGLISH AS A SECOND F*CKING LANGUAGE.

ESFL University Press, 1995. ISBN 0-9644545-0-5

DEPRAVED AND INSULTING ENGLISH.

Harvest books, 2002. ISBN 0156011492

COP SPEAK: THE LINGO OF LAW ENFORCEMENT AND CRIME.

John Wiley & Sons, 1996. ISBN 0-471-04304-4

NTC'S AMERICAN IDIOMS DICTIONARY.

National Textbook Co., 1988. Library of Congress Number: 86-63996

SLANG AND EUPHEMISM: A DICTIONARY OF OATHS, CURSES, INSULTS, SEXUAL AND METAPHOR, RACIAL SLURS, DRUG TALK, HOMOSEXUAL LINGO, AND RELATED MATTERS. *Jonathan David, 1981.*

FORBIDDEN AMERICAN ENGLISH.

McGraw-Hill/Contemporary Books, 1990. ISBN 0844251496

Online Slang Dictionaries

The Alternative English Dictionary

http://www.notam02.co/~hcholm/altlang/ht/English.html

Commonly-Used American Slang

http://www.manythings.org/slang/

Cool Western Slang

http://www.bible.org/western_slang.html

Gay Slang Dictionary

http://www.hurricane.net/~wizard/19a.html

Online Dictionary of Street Drug Slang

http://www.drugs.indiana.edu/slang/home.html

Recent Slang

http://www.slangsite.com/

Slang Dictionary

http://members.tripod.com/~jaguarpage/slang.htm

Tru Dat

http://members.tripod.com/~mara_juarez/slang.htm

Vox Dictionary of Contemporary Slang

http://www.lexscripta.com/desktop/dictionaries/slang.html

Essential Dictionaries and other Reference Materials for Court Interpreters and Translators

English Monolingual Dictionaries

American Heritage Dictionary of the English Language, 4th Edition
> Format: Hardcover, 4th ed., 2116pp.
> ISBN: 035825172
> Publisher: Houghton Mifflin Company
> Pub. Date: September 2000
> Edition Desc: 4th

Random House Webster's Unabridged Dictionary
> Format: Hardcover, 3rd ed., 2256pp.
> ISBN: 0375425667
> Publisher: Random House Information Group
> Pub. Date: September 2001
> Edition Desc: 2nd

Black's Law Dictionary (American and English Jurisprudence)
> Format: Textbook Hardcover, 7th ed., 1776pp
> ISBN: 0314228640
> Publisher: West Group
> Pub. Date: August 1999

Dictionaries for Languages other than English

ARABIC

Al Mawrid (English-Arabic/Arabic-English dictionary)
> Format: Hardcover, 3rd ed., 2376pp
> ASIN: 1894412974
> Publisher: Dar El Ilm Lilmalayin
> Pub. Date: March 1998

Al Mawrid 2002: A Modern English-Arabic Dictionary
> Format: Hardcover
> ISBN: 9953900426
> Publisher: Librarie Du Moyen-Orient
> Pub. Date: 2001

Arabic-English Faruqi's Law Dictionary
> Format: Hardcover, 3rd ed., 380pp.
> ISBN: 0884310728
> Publisher: I B D Ltd
> Pub. Date: December 1986
> (This dictionary is also available in English-Arabic)

CHINESE

Chinese-English Dictionary
> Format: Hardcover, 1401pp.
> ISBN: 962-04-0398-3
> Pub. Date: 1991

English-Chinese Dictionary
> Format: Hardcover, 1769pp.
> ISBN: 962-04-0201-4
> Pub. Date: 1991

Chinese-English New Practical Dictionary
>   Format: Paperback, 1418pp.
>   ISBN: 0-88431-193-7
>   Pub. Date: 1987

Chinese-English (Mandarin) Dictionary
>   Format: Hardcover, 660pp.
>   ISBN: 0-88431-261-5
>   Pub. Date: 1967

English –Chinese Glossary of American Criminal Law
>   Format: Paperback, 246pp.
>   ISBN: 0-88727-111-1
>   Pub. Date: 1989

English-Cantonese Glossary
>   Format: Looseleaf
>   ISBN: N/A
>   Pub. Date: N/A

Glossary of Selected Legal Terms English-Cantonese
>   Office of the Administrator of the Courts, State of Washington
>   Distributed by ACEBO, P.O. Box 7485, CA 93962

FRENCH

Dictionnaire Encyclopedique, 2 vols
>   Format: Hardcover, 2124 pp.
>   ISBN: 2-03-301806-1
>   Pub. Date: 1994

Le Nouveau Petit Robert: Dictionnaire De La Langue Francaise
>   Format : Hardcover
>   ISBN : 2850368261
>   Publisher : Le Robert
>   Pub. Date : 2002

Harper Collins Robert French Unabridged Dictionary
>
> Format: Hardcove, 6th ed., 2142pp.
>
> ISBN: 0060084502
>
> Publisher: Harper Resource
>
> Pub. Date: 2002

GREEK

Greek-English Dictionary, 2 vols
>
> Format: Hardcover, 1318 pp.
>
> ISBN: 0-88431-922-9
>
> Pub. Date: 1961

English-Greek Dictionary
>
> Format: Hardcover, 1102 pp.
>
> ISBN: 0-88431-125-2
>
> Pub. Date: 1961

HAITIAN CREOLE

Haitian Creole-English-French Dictionary
>
> Deslan Creole-English-French Dictionary
>
> 22-11 Church Ave
>
> Brooklyn, NY 11226
>
> (718) 693-0461

Haitian Creole-English-French Dictionary
>
> 1981, Bloomington Indiana-Creole Institute
>
> Haitiana Publications
>
> 170-08 Hillside Ave.
>
> Jamaica, NY 11432
>
> (718) 523-0135

Haitian Creole-English Dictionary
>
> Targetej, Dunwoody Press
>
> ISBN 0-93174575-6

ITALIAN

Italian Encyclopedia Universal Dictionary
> Format: Hardcover, 1860 pp.
> ISBN: 88-7166-174-5

Italian-English English-Italian Dictionary (Sansoni)
> ISBN: 88-3831437-3

English-Italian Law Dictionary
> ISBN: 88-1400316-5
> Pub. Date: 1994

Italian-English Law Dictionary
> ISBN: 88-1405001-5
> Pub. Date: 1996

KOREAN

Korean-English Dictionary
> Format: Flex, 2182 pp.
> ISBN: 89-387-04020-5
> Publisher: Minjungseorim
> Pub. Date: 1994

English-Korean Dictionary
> Format: Flex; 2687 pp.
> ISBN: 89-387-0401-7
> Publisher: Minjung
> Pub. Date: 1994

English-Korean Glossary
> Format: Looseleaf
> ISBN: N/A
> Publisher: ACEBO
> Pub. Date: N/A

POLISH

The Great Polish/English Dictionary (2 Volume set)
Format: Hardcover; 1728 pp.
ISBN: 83-214-0956-3
Pub. Date: 1992

The Great English/Polish Dictionary
Format: Hardcover; 1404 pp.
ISBN: 83-214-0955-5
Pub. Date: 1992

Polish/English Dictionary of Legal Terms
ISBN: H3-04-01897-7

English/Polish Dictionary of Legal and Economic Terms
Format: Hardcover; 724 pp.
ISBN: 83-214-0533-9
Pub. Date: 1991

Kodeks Karny- Postepowania Karnego
ISBN: 83-85330-30-5

Kodeks Cywilny-Kodeks Postepowania Cywilnego
ISBN: 83-9004443-3-1

PORTUGUESE

Portuguese Dictionary-Novo
ISBN: 85-209-0411-4

Pequeño Diccionario Enciclopedia Koogan Larousse
Editorial Larousse do Brasil, Rio de Janeiro
Imported Books. P.O. Box 4414, Dallas Texas
(214) 941-6497

Dictionary Portuguese-English (2 Volumes)
Format: Hardcover; 1328 pp.
ISBN: 85-06-01598-7

English-Portuguese Dictionary
Format: Hardcover; 1151 pp.
ISBN: 85-06-01599-5

Diccionario Juridico, 3rd edition
Maria Chaves de Mello. Rio de Janeiro: Barrister's Editors, 1987

Noronha's Legal Dictionary
Durval de Noronha Goyos, Jr.
Sao Paulo: Editora Observador Legal, 1993

RUSSIAN

Russian Encyclopedia Dictionary
Format: Hardcover; 1632 pp.
ISBN: 5-85270-001-0

English-Russian Dictionary 2 Volumes
Format: Hardcover; 2108 pp.
ISBN: 0-88431-168-6
Pub. Date: 1988

Russian-English Translator's Dictionary
Format: Hardcover; 735 pp.
ISBN: 0-471-93316-3
Pub. Date: 1991

Russian-English Legal Dictionary
ISBN: 5-88746-004-0

English-Russian Dictionary of American Criminal Law
>ISBN: 0-313-30455-6
>Available from Greenwood Publishing Group
>P.O. Box 5007, Westport, CT 06881-5007

SPANISH

Diccionario de la Lengua Española
>ISBN: 84-239-4399-2

Diccionario de Uso del Español (2 volumes)
>ISBN: 84-249-1344-2

Larousse Gran Diccionario
>Español-Ingles/Ingles- Español
>ISBN: 970-607-023-0

Simon and Schuster International Dictionary
>English-Spanish/Spanish-English
>ISBN: 0-671-21507-8 plain edition
>ISBN: 0-671-21267-2 thumb-indexed

Unabridged Spanish Dictionary
>Harper Collins

Diccionario Juridico Español-Ingles
>Guillermo Cabanellas de las Cuevas and Eleanor C. Hoague.
>Editorial Heliasta, 1998

Diccionario De Términos Jurídicos Ingles-Español, Spanish-English
>Format: Hardcover; 688 pp.
>ISBN: 84-344-0506-7
>Pub. Date: 1995

Bilingual Dictionary of Criminal Justice Terms (English-Spanish)
      ISBN: 0-87526-379-8
      The Interpreter's Companion, 4th Edition
      ACEBO, P.O. Box 7485, Spreckels, CA 93962
      (Contains six separate Spanish-English, English-Spanish glossaries: Legal Terms, Traffic and Automotive Terms, Drug Terms, Weapons   Terms, Medical Terms, and Slang Terms)

VIETNAMESE

Vietnamese-English/English-Vietnamese Dictionary
      Format: Hardcover; 826 pp.
      ISBN: 0-88431-113-9
      Pub. Date: 1992

English-Vietnamese Glossary
      Format: Looseleaf
      ISBN: N/A
      Publisher: ACEBO
      Pub. Date: N/A

BOOK DISTRIBUTORS

For All Languages

Imported Books
2025 West Clarendon
P.O. Box 4414
Dallas, TX 75208
(214) 941-6497

i.b.d, Ltd.
International Book Distributors
24 Hudson St
Kinderhook, NY 12106
(800) 343-35312

Schoenhof's Foreign Books
76A Mount Auburn Street
Cambridge, MA 02138
(617) 547-8855

United Nations Bookstore
G.A. 32 New York, NY 10017
(212) 963-7680

French, German, Italian, Portuguese and Spanish

Europa Books
Evanston, IL 60201
(708) 886-6262

Spanish books

Ediciones Universal
P.O. Box 450353
Miami, FL 33245-0353
(305) 642-3234

OTHER RESOURCES

American Translators Association (ATA)
225 Reinekers Lane, Suite 590
Alexandria, VA 22314
(703) 683-6100
ata@atanet.org
http://www.atanet.org/
A national not-for-profit association established in 1959, ATA has over 6,500 members throughout the US and abroad. Among its professional activities, it holds an annual conference every fall, publishes as monthly magazine, The ATA Chronicle, and offers accreditation in several language pairs.

The American Association of Language Specialists (TAALS)
http://www.taals.net/

Berlitz
Interpreter Training and Quality Assurance
Bowne Global Solutions
1730 Rhode Island Ave NW, Suite 308
Washington, DC 20036
800-423-6756 x. 180
dawn.birnie@bowneglobal.net
www.bowneglobal.com
A variety of seminars are offered for interpreters of all languages, both on site and via distance learning.

Distance Opportunities for Interpreter Training (DO IT) Center
1059 Alton Way, Box 7
Denver, CO 80230
http://au.frcc.cccoes.edu/~doit/
The DO IT Center has traditionally offered the following courses:

Diagnostic Assessment and Skills Training Series
This is a yearlong series comprised of three courses. Self-instructional packets will lead students through structured skill development activities targeting individual needs. WebCT will serve as the online classroom for discussion and collaborations during the completion of self-instructional materials.

Prior Learning Assessment
This 15-week online course introduces you to the process of creating a professional portfolio and provides you with the opportunity you with the opportunity to systematically collect materials that effectively demonstrate the knowledge and skills you have developed.

Interpreting in the American Legal System

This online course is comprised of four courses distributed over four semesters. A one-week onsite supervised practicum in Denver, CO is associated with the final course.

*You must meet your state's requirements to interpreter in legal settings to apply for these courses.

National Association of Judiciary Interpreters and Translators (NAJIT)

603 Stewart St., Suite 610
Seattle, Washington 98101
Tel: 206-267-2300
headquarters@najit.org
http://www.najit.org/

New York University School of Continuing and Professional Studies

The American Language Institute
NYU School of Continuing and Professional Studies
48 Cooper Square, Room 200
New York, NY 10003
(212) 998-7200
scpsinfo@nyu.edu
http://www.scps.nyu.edu/ali

Northwest Translators and Interpreters Society (NOTIS)

P.O. Box 25301
Seattle, WA 98165-2201 USA
(206) 382-5642
Info@notisnet.org
http://www.notisnet.org

Registry of Interpreters for the Deaf (RID)

333 Commerce Street
Alexandria, VA 22314
(703) 838-0030 V
(703) 838-0459 TTY
http://www.rid.org/

Rutgers, Faculty of Arts and Sciences Continuing Education (FASCE)

FASCE Corporate Program, Tillet 107
Rutgers, The State University of New Jersey
53 Avenue E
Piscataway, NJ 08854-8040
(732) 932-5937

http://fasce.rutgers.edu/eslce.htm

FASCE offers courses in accent improvement for persons who have a strong command and fluency in English, but who wish to increase their intelligibility in English. Courses are scheduled BY ARRANGEMENT and registrations are accepted at any time.

American English Accent Improvement, FAS-470
American English Accent Improvement Tutorial, FAS-471
American English Accent Improvement Tutorial, FAS-472

FASCE offers other courses for professional development in spoken English as a second language:

Speaking English Professionally
Vocabulary and Grammar for Effective Speech
Presentation Skills for Nonnative Speakers of English
Speech and Accent Assessment

The Translators and Interpreters Guild (TTIG)

http://www.ttig.org/

Washington State Court Interpreters and Translators Society (WITS)
http://witsnet.org/

Society of Medical Interpreters (SOMI)
http://www.sominet.org/

Northern California Translators Association (NCTA)
http://www.ncta.org/

California Court Interpreters Association (CCIA)
http://www.ccia.org/

Southern California Area Translators and Interpreters Association (SCATIA)
http://www.scatia.org/

Colorado Translators Association (CTA)
http://www.cta-web.org/

New Mexico Translators and Interpreters Association (NMTIA)
http://internet.cybermesa.com/~nmtia/

Austin Area Translators and Interpreters Association (AATIA)
http://www.aatia.org/

El Paso Interpreters and Translators Association (EPITA)
1003 Alethea Pl.
El Paso, TX 79902,
Email: grdelgado@aol.com

Huston Interpreters and Translators Association (HITA)
P.O. Box 61285
Huston, TX, 77208-1285
(713) 935-2123

Indiana Supreme Court Commission on Race and Gender Fairness Sub-Committee on Language and Cultural Issues:
A Judge's Reference Guide to Language Interpretation in Indiana Courts
http://www.in.gov/judiciary/fairness/pubs/interp-benchbook.pdf

Metroplex Interpreters and Translators Association (MTIA)
http://www.dfw-mita.com/

Upper Midwest Translators and Interpreters Association (UMTIA)
Minnesota Translation Laboratory
218 Nolte Center
315 Pillsbury Drive SE
Minneapolis, MN 55455, (612) 625-3096
Email: Laurence.h.bogoslaw-1@tc.umn.edu

Nebraska Association of Translators and Interpreters (NATI)
http://www.natihg.org/

Saint Louis Translators and Interpreters (SLTIN)
P.O. Box 3722
Balwin, MO 63022-3722
(314) 394-5334

Chicago Area Translators/Interpreters Network (CHICATA)
http://www.chicata.org/

Michigan Translators/Interpreters Network (MiTiN)
http://www.mitinweb.org/

Northeast Ohio Translators Association (NOTA)
http://www.ohiotranslators.org/

The Kentucky Translators and Interpreters Association (KTIA)
P.O. Box 7468
Louisville, KY 40257-0468 (502) 548-3988
email: vapues@insightbb.com

Tennessee Association of Professional Interpreters and Translators (TAPIT)
http://www.tapit.org/

Carolina Association of Translators and Interpreters (CATI)
http://www.catiweb.org/

Atlanta Association of Interpreters and Translators (AAIT)
http://www.aait.org/

Florida Chapter of the American Translators Association (FLATA)
http://www.atafl.org/

Delaware Valley Translators Association (DVTA)
http://www.dtva.org/

Massachusetts Medical Interpreters Association (MMIA)
http://diversityrx.org/HTML/MOASSA.htm

New England Translators Association (NETA)
http://www.netaweb.org/

New York Circle of Translators (NYCT)
http://www.nyctranslators.org/

References for Spanish Interpreters & Translators

Spanish-English Dictionaries
Oxford Spanish-English Dictionary
Harper-Collins Spanish-English Dictionary
American Heritage Larousse Spanish-English Dictionary
Simon & Schuster's International Dictionary
Larousse Spanish-English Dictionary

General Language References
Diccionario de ideas afines, by Fernando Corrio, pub. Editorial Herder.
Diccionario de dudad y dificultades de la lengua Española, by Manuel Seco, pub. Espasa Calpe
Diccionario de uso del español, by Maria Moliner, pub. Editorial Gredos
Using Spanish Synonyms, by R.E. Bachelor, pub. Cambridge University Press
Diccionario razonado de sinonimos y contrarios, by Jose M. Zainqui, pub. Editorial de Vecchi
NTC Dictionary of Spanish False Cognates, pub. National Textbook Company

Legal Dictionaries
Butterworth's English-Spanish Dictionary, by Cabanellas & Hoague, pub. *Butterwort*
West's Spanish-English/English-Spanish Law Dictionary, by Solis & Gasteazoro, Pub. West
Diccionario de derecho, by Pina y Pina Vera, pub. Porrua
Bilingual Dictionary of Criminal Justice Terms, by Benmaman, Connolly & Loos, pub. Gould
Diccionario de terminos juridicos, by Hughes and Alcaraz Varo, pub. Ariel

Mail-order Bookstores

Imported Books

P.O. Box 4414

Dallas, TX 75208

(214) 941-6497

InTrans Book Service

P.O. Box 467

Kinderhook, NY 12106

(518) 758-1755

FAX (518) 758-6702

www.intransbooks.com

lankhof@intransbooks.com

Western Continental Book, Inc.

625 E. 70th Ave., #5

Denver, CO 80229

(303) 289-1761

Libreria de Porrua Hnos. y Cia, S.A

Apartado M-7990

Delegacion Cuauhtemoc

06020, Mexico, D.F.

Tels. 702-45-74 y 702-49-34

Fax 702-65-29 y 702-45-74 ext. 140

porrua.com.mx

References of Regional & Colloquial Spanish

Regional Spanish

Argentina

Academia Argentina de Letras. Diccionario del habla de los argentinos. Espasa, 2003. ISBN 950-852-152-X Dis, Emilio. Codigo Lunfardo, Editorial Cabure, 1975.

Escobar, Raúl Tomas. Diccionario del hampa y del delito: lunfardo Latinoamericano, drogadicción, "punk", insurrección, mitología, voces vulgares y Populares. Editorial Universidad, 1986.

Feldman Rosa, Jorge O. New Dictionary of Dirty Words/Nuevo diccionario de malas Palabras. Info, 1996. ISBN 987-95820-0-4

Gobello, José. Nuevo diccionario lunfardo. Ediciones Corregidor, 1994. ISBN 950-05-0565-8

Chile

Subercaseaux, Miguel. Diccionario de chilenismos. Editorial Juvenil, 1986.

Costa Rica

Pacheco, Miguel Q. Nuevo diccionario de costarriqueñismos. Publisher Unknown. ISBN 9977660557

Cuba

Sanchez-Boudy, José. Diccionario de Cubanismo más usuales (Como habla el cubano). Ediciones Universal, 1978. ISBN 0-89729-199-9

El Salvador

Geoffroy Rivas, Pedro. El español que hablamos en El Salvador. Ministerio de Educación, Dirección de Publicaciones, San Salvador, El Salvador, 1982.

Latin America

Lipski, John M. Latin American Spanish. Longman, 1994. ISBN 0-58208-760-0

Mexico

Cabrera, Luis. Diccionario de Aztequismos. Editorial Oasis, 1975.

Galvan, Roberto A. and Teschener, Richard V. El diccionario del español chicano National Textbook Company, 1985 ISBN 0-8325-9634-5

Gomez de Silva, Guido. *Diccionario Breve de Mexicanismos. Academia Mexicana, Fondo de Cultura Económica, 2001. Hamel's Bilingual Dictionary of Mexican Spanish. Bilingual Book Press, 1994. ISBN 1-886835-01-4*

Mejia Prieto, Jorge. *Asi habla el mexicano: Diccionario basico de mexicanismos. Panorama Editorial, S.A., 1984. ISBN 968-38-0122-6*

Robinson, Linton H. *Mexican Slang: A ¡*#@%&+! Guide. Bueno Books, 1992. ISBN 0-9627080-7-0*

Perú

Bendezu Neyra, Guillermo E. *Argot Limeño o Jerga Criolla del Peru Editorial Lima, S.A., no date. De Arona. Juan. Diccionario de peruanismos. Biblioteca Peruana, 1975.*

Puerto Rico

Altieri de Barreto, Carmen G. *El Lexico de la Delincuencia en Puerto Rico. Editorial Universitaria, Universidad de Puerto Rico, 1973.*

Gallo, Cristino. *Language of the Puerto Rico Street: A Slang Dictionary with English Cross-Reference. Book Service of Puerto Rico, 1980.*

Llorens, Washington. *El habla popular de Puerto Rico. Editorial Edil, 1974.*

Spain

Leon, Victor. *Diccionario de argot español. Alianza Editorial, 1988. ISBN 84-206-1766-0*

Slang and Colloquial Usage

Berger, Frances de Talavera. *¡Mierda! The Real Spanish You Were Never Taught in School. Plume, 1990. ISBN 0-452-26424-3*

Burke, David. *Street Spanish: How to Speak and Understand Spanish Slang. John Wiley & Sons, Inc., 1991. ISBN 0-471-52846-3*

Burke, David. *Street Spanish Slang Dictionary & Thesaurus. John Wiley & Sons, Inc.,1999. ISBN 0-471-16834-3*

Cruz, Bill and Teck, Bill. *The Official Spanglish Dictionary. Fireside- Simon & Schuster, 1998. ISBN 0-7641-0619-8*

Mahler. Michael. *Dictionary of Spanish Slang and Colloquial Expressions. Barrons, 2000. ISBN 0-7641-0619-8*

Pierson, Raymond H. Guide to Spanish Idioms. Passport Books, 1992. ISBN 0-8442-7325-2

Polkinhorn, Harry; Velasco, Alfredo; and Lambert, Malcom. El libro de calo. Floricante Press, 1988.

Rosensweig, Jay B. Caló: Gutter Spanish. n & Co., ISBN 0-525-47436-7

Regional Spanish Websites

Diccionarios de variantes del español
http://www3.unileon.es/dp/dfh/jmr/dicci/007.htm

Dialectología Española
http://www.tulane.edu/~spanling/Dial/DialEsp.html

Ecuador

http://www.lenguaje.com/

Mexico

http://www.academia.org.mx/dbm/DICAZ/a.htm
http://mexico.udg.mx/arte/folclore/picardia/

Puerto Rico

http://www.geocities.com/SouthBeach/Castle/1496/dicc.html

Republica Dominicana

http://usuarios.lycos.es/jallite/toolbar.htm

Venezuela

http://www.lenguaje.com/

Self-Help Training Resources

ACEBO

P.O. Box 7485

Spreckels, CA 93962

(831) 455-1507

http://www.acebo.com

Agnes Haury Institute for court interpretation

University of Arizona

Modern Languages Bldg. #67, Room 445

Tucson, AZ 95721

(520) 621-3685

http://nci.arizona.edu/ahi.shtml

Alicia Ernand Productions

P.O. Box 802382

Santa Clarita, CA 91380-2382

(661) 296-4682

http://www.aliciaernand.com/

The NCRA Store

The National Court Reporters Association

8224 Old Courthouse Road

Vienna, VA 22182-3808

800-272-6272

http://www.ncraonline.org

Reference Materials

THE BILINGUAL COURTROOM: COURT INTERPRETERS IN THE JUDICIAL PROCESS, (with a new chapter), 2002. University of Chicago Press, 1427 East 60th Street, Chicago, IL 60637. www.press.uchicago.edu

INTERPRETERS AND THE LEGAL PROCESS. Winchester: Waterside Press, 1996. Available from the publisher at www.watersidepress.com.uk

THE ART OF LEGAL INTERPRETATION. Continuing Education Press, Portland State University, P.O. Box 1394, Portland, OR 97207-1394. www.cep.pdx.edu

AN INTRODUCTION TO COURT INTERPRETING: THEORY & PRACTICE, 1992. University Press of America, Inc., 4720 Boston Way, Lanham, MD 20706. www.univpress.com

THE PRACTICE OF COURT INTERPRETING, 1995. John Benjamins North America, P.O. Box 27519, Philadelphia PA 19118. www.benjamins.com

FUNDAMENTALS OF COURT INTERPRETATION: THEORY, POLICY AND PRACTICE. Carolina Academic Press, 700 Kent Street, Durham, NC 27701. www.cappress.com

COURT INTERPRETATION: MODEL GUIDES FOR POLICY AND PRACTICE IN THE STATE COURTS. Williamsburg, VA: National Center for State Courts, 1995. This book is out of print, but it can be downloaded from www.ncsonline.org

INTRODUCTION TO COURT INTERPRETING, 2000.
http://www.intransbooks.com

INTRODUCTION TO JUDICIARY INTERPRETING. National Association of Judiciary Interpreters and Translators, 2150 N. 107th St., Suite 205 Seattle, WA 98133. http://www.najit.org/

PROTEUS, THE NEWSLETTER OF THE NATIONAL ASSOCIATION OF JUDICIARY INTERPRETERS AND TRANSLATORS. http://www.najit.org/proteus/proteus.html

COURT INTERPRETERS: STANDARDS OF PRACTICE AND STANDARDS FOR TRAINING. *Cornell Journal of Law and Public Policy.* 6 (3), Spring 1997, 645-672.

Information Source: Indiana State Certification Training Manual-2008

www.DESOTOTRANSLATIONS.com